MIXED BLESSINGS

MIXED BLESSINGS

My Psychic Life

Diane Lazarus

Century · London

Published by Century 2007

4 6 8 10 9 7 5 3

First published in Great Britain in 2007 by
Century
Random House, 20 Vauxhall Bridge Road,
London SW1V 2SA

www.randomhouse.co.uk

Addresses for companies within The Random House Group Limited can
be found at: www.randomhouse.co.uk/offices.htm

The Random House Group Limited Reg. No. 954009

A CIP catalogue record for this book
is available from the British Library

ISBN 9781846052019

Mixed Sources
Product group from well-managed
forests and other controlled sources
www.fsc.org Cert no. TT-COC-2139
© 1996 Forest Stewardship Council
FSC

Typeset by SX Composing DTP, Rayleigh, Essex
Printed and bound in Great Britain by
Mackays of Chatham plc, Chatham, Kent

For my great, great grandfather, Ronald Owen
Preston; for Mark Green for his proof of survival;
for my wonderful healing angel Jayne
and for all my spirit friends.

Acknowledgements

A big thank you to Linda Dearsley for her time, patience, wonderful way with words and her natural ability to write fast!

I would like to thank Hannah Black at Random House for using her intuition and believing that this would make an interesting book; Karolina Sutton of ICM Talent for her patience; my one and only best friend and sister, Debbie, for reminding me of things long forgotten and for encouraging me to develop my gift; my brother Gary whom I most respect, who was always there for me, caught fish for my supper and – not surprisingly – went on to become Welsh International Fly Fishing champion 2006–7.

I would like to say a special thank you to ex policeman Peter Hall for his faith in me and my gift. Also thanks to Mr Bob Hinton, criminologist and author, for giving me the chance to prove to myself and others that spirits will not rest until there has been justice. And a big thank you from the bottom of my heart to ex CID officer, Marcela Daly, for giving Mark Green the chance to prove he would see justice done through me.

I would also like to mention the following people: Mr and Mrs Green, Mark's parents; Myron, Mark's aunt; Jayne's sister Denise and her two lovely sons; Clive's daughter Clare, and Marlene, my special auntie. Thank you all. Without your blessing this book would not have been possible. And thank you to everyone else mentioned in this book, you know who you are! Bless you x.

Finally a big thank you to my wonderful husband and soul mate, Peter, who has been my tower of strength throughout my career; and my two lovely, gifted children Lisa and Liam for waiting so patiently while I was locked in my study.

Most importantly, thank you to my unique, irreplaceable mother who brought me into the world against all the odds, maybe in order for me to write this book and to share with the world that life goes on . . .

Chapter One

He was there again.

Even with my eyes tightly shut and the bedclothes pulled right over my head I could feel his presence. Over there in the corner, crouched low in the shadows, he was waiting, waiting for me . . .

I lay rigid, muscles locked, ears straining, fingers gripping the covers so hard the pink candlewick left snakey tracks across my palm.

Silence. Somewhere a door banged. Out in the field the wind shook the trees. The glass in the window rattled.

He was still there, I was sure of it. Sweat prickled the roots of my hair. I didn't want to, but I had to look. Cautiously, I prised open my eyes. There against the wall I could see a denser patch of blackness; a solid shape where no solid shape had any business to be. Then the curtains twisted in the breeze, a band of moonlight fell across the room and suddenly a ghastly face leapt silver-white out of the dark. It was a face all seamed and criss-crossed with lines – a face somehow *made* of lines. And then the lined mouth opened, the colourless lips started to move – and all at once I was screaming.

I was up and out of bed and across the room in one movement, screaming through the door, screaming down the hall, screaming straight into my mother's arms.

'Hey! There, there. It's all right, baby, it's all right.' She was rocking me, stroking my hair as my tears soaked her nightie, 'Whatever's the matter? Not that dream again? It was only a dream baby. Only a dream.'

But it wasn't a dream. I may have been barely four years old but I knew the difference between a dream and reality. And that man was real. And he came to my room every night.

* * *

I was the child that wasn't meant to be – as far as my father was concerned, anyway. Maybe that accounted for my strange ways. As least that's what Mum often thought, and it worried her greatly; for she was harbouring a secret guilt. Every day my mother lived with the knowledge of what had happened before I was born, and she knew it hadn't been right.

When my father heard that my mother was expecting for the fourth time he didn't rush out to buy champagne and cigars to celebrate my imminent arrival; he didn't throw his arms around her in a big hug of pride and delight: no, Dad walked silently out and made instead for the corner shop where he stocked up on boxes and boxes of mustard powder. Goodness knows where he got the idea, something he'd heard in the army perhaps, but he came home, ran a scalding bath and tipped in all the sulphur-bright dust.

'Funny smell,' thought Mum as she passed the door and heard the taps running full blast. The next second she was dragged inside and ordered into the foaming tub. And as my mother sat there in the yellow water, eyes streaming through a fog of steam and pungent fumes, Dad thrust a tumbler of gin into her boiled-lobster hand.

'I'll lose the baby, Alastair!' she protested, trying to push it away, but he just shoved the glass roughly to her lips and forced her to drink.

'You can't have another baby,' he snarled. 'We can't manage the ones we've got.'

A whole bottle later, Mum was finally allowed out of the bath. Scarlet, sore, gin-fuddled and tear-stained she staggered down the hall and collapsed, despairing, into bed. When she woke the next day she had the worst hangover of her life but, amazingly, she still had me. Even in the womb it seemed, I was determined to defy my father.

Dad wasn't one to give up easily, however. 'You can't have this baby,' he kept saying, 'we can't afford three, let alone four.' So he hit on a new idea.

My father had discovered that one of our neighbours couldn't have children and, desperate for a family, she'd applied to an adoption agency for a baby – preferably a dark-haired boy since she and her husband had always wanted a son and, coming from Tanzania, they were both dark themselves. But adoption was a frustrating business. The whole process could take a very long time and no-one could predict when a suitable infant might become available. It could be years before she held a baby of her own in her arms and the situation was causing her great sadness.

My father was all sympathetic concern. 'Don't worry,' he told her, with the charming smile he could summon from some secret place deep inside when it was worth his while, 'if Pat's still pregnant you can adopt our baby. We've got enough children already. Really.'

He was completely serious and the woman took him at his word. It must have seemed to her the perfect solution. Both my parents happened to have hair as black as coal and were highly likely to produce a dark baby. And having been blessed with so many children already, she probably reasoned, they could easily spare one of their brood, especially if money was tight.

'But not a word to Pat just yet,' my father warned. 'You know what pregnant women are like – over-emotional.'

Our neighbour nodded understandingly and solemnly promised to avoid the subject. But she hadn't promised to avoid Mum. Shortly afterwards my mother was perplexed to find that her previously casual acquaintance was on the doorstep almost every day, apparently overcome with concern for Mum's health. She insisted on helping with the chores and regularly minding my brother Gary, and toddler sister Debbie. 'Get some rest, Pat,' she'd urge, steering Mum to the settee. 'You've got to put your feet up now and then, for the baby's sake.'

Unknown to Mum, when our neighbour wasn't in

our flat dusting and polishing, she was catching the bus into town to stock up on all the sweet little baby clothes, nappies and rattles of which she'd been dreaming for so long. Without a word to anyone, she stored them away in a special cupboard ready for the great day when Mum produced the promised child.

Although she didn't know the full story, Mum became increasingly baffled. She sensed there was something going on behind her back and, though she couldn't imagine what it was, she became more and more apprehensive. With good reason, as it turned out, because apparently my father was even trying to get hold of adoption papers to make the whole clandestine transaction legal.

But at the last minute his hopes were dashed again. Just one week before I was due, our neighbour received the good news that the adoption agency had found her a perfect little boy.

Out came all the hoarded infant treasures from the special cupboard and, completely forgetting about me, the woman and her husband hurried away for the joyful collection of their brand new son, Thomas.

How my father must have fumed. Mum was tremendously relieved, although she couldn't exactly say why, but her troubles weren't quite over yet. Vindictive to the last, Dad made one final attempt to thwart my arrival. When Mum's waters broke the following Friday, Dad refused to allow her to seek medical help and sent her to bed. All that weekend he ignored her tears and pleading but finally by Monday, when she was screaming in pain and likely to have the neighbours calling round with the police, he agreed to let the midwife call. Dad wouldn't allow her to go to hospital because he said he wasn't going to be left to care for three kids.

The midwife was shocked when she saw the state Mum was in. 'I'm sorry, I hate to say this to people,' she said with a grim expression on her face after examining Mum, 'but you've got to prepare yourself for a stillborn.'

Yet to her astonishment, a little while later this scrawny, scarlet scrap with big dark eyes and an indignant scream came kicking into the world. Apparently I arrived clenching my tiny fists so tightly my sharp little nails had dug deep into my palms leaving a neat row of red cuts along the inside of my hands.

The midwife was amazed that I was breathing at all, but delighted. 'You've got a little boxer here!' she said, handing me over to my exhausted mum.

It was Tuesday October 19 1965 and against all the odds I'd made it. But, although she didn't know it then, it was to be the last time Mum would ever hold her own newborn child in her arms. Dad saw to that.

That day, of course, she was more than content to count her blessings. She was so grateful that I was alive, and had entered the world with a complete set of limbs and no obvious signs of damage, that she blotted out from her mind all the difficulties of the past few months. But everyone wanted to know what I was to be called. They couldn't refer to me as Baby Preston, they said. I had to have a name. Surely Mum and Dad had discussed it? How could Mum, lying exhausted in her room surrounded by a few thoughtful flowers from friends, say that my father, who was still sulking, wasn't interested? So she cast about for a name. A few years earlier, the record 'Diana' had been very big in the charts and it was one of Mum's favourite songs. What a pretty name, she'd thought at the time, and now it sprang into her mind. But just in case 'Diana' was a little too reminiscent of the fifties' hit, she swapped the final 'a' for an 'e'. So Diane I became and it wasn't long before Mum was able to load me into our old-fashioned pram and wheel me round the district, showing off the latest addition to the Preston family still bearing a passing resemblance to a prize-fighter.

The mythical Diana, of course, was a goddess, but as the months went on it began to look as if the infant Diane was more of a little devil. I was a troublesome child. Small for my age, with tangled dark hair and enormous brown eyes that seemed too large for my pointed little face, I clung to Mum like a skinny white limpet and made a big drama if she left me alone for one second.

I was a great puzzle to her. Since I was the youngest of four she could understand that I might feel overlooked and may take to inventing wild stories for attention, but what she couldn't fathom, though, was why, from the age of about two, I should suffer such terrible nightmares that sent me hurtling out of bed night after night. My terror was obviously not faked for effect and something seemed to be very wrong. Mum couldn't help wondering if my father's clumsy attempts to terminate the pregnancy had led to some invisible, but serious, damage after all. The real reason, of course, would never have entered her head.

We lived on the fourth floor of a lone tower block on the edge of Swansea. Across the road was a windy hillside of spindly trees and scrubby grass; behind lay the mountains and in front the steep streets tumbled down and down towards the docks and the sea.

On winter nights storms howled around our stubby tower, strange sounds sighed through gaps in the window frames and rain hurled itself against the glass like bullets. Yet what went on inside the flat was much more frightening to me than anything outside. As a small child I was confused. Other people seemed to live in our home besides the six of us, but they appeared to be engaged in a perpetual, one-sided game of hide-and-seek. Whenever you approached they darted away before you could catch a glimpse of them. If you turned your head quickly you just caught an impression of movement, as if someone had scurried swiftly behind you.

And the place was never silent. Sometimes as I passed the lounge the sound of children laughing and giggling would be coming from inside and I'd throw open the door expecting to see my brother and sister playing there – but the room was deserted and the bare, parquet floor gleamed emptily.

At other times I'd hear girls arguing in my brother Gary's room when I was quite certain the others were out at school. I'd tiptoe up and peer inside, but instantly the voices died away and there was no-one there. Unnerved, I'd back out and run screaming for Mum.

They never slept, these invisible people who shared our flat. At night when I went to bed, the unseen chatterers just increased the volume. One voice in particular was always louder and more persistent than the others. It was a man's voice but he had a very odd way of speaking. Years later, walking down the street I heard the exact same accent floating across from a group of young people. They told me they came from Liverpool. So although I didn't know it at the time, my regular visitor was Liverpudlian.

'Don't worry,' he used to say to me in his funny voice, 'I'm protecting you. I'm looking after you. Everything's going to be all right. You're safe.'

This should have been reassuring, but it wasn't. His voice sounded so strange and foreign to me and I didn't understand what he meant. Why did he need to look after me? Why wasn't I safe? And most of all, why couldn't I see him and how had he got into my bedroom? 'Go away!' I'd yell, petrified. And for a while he'd back off and there'd be silence, but he always returned.

'Debbie, that man's talking to me again,' I used to tell my older sister who lay curled up above me in her cosy bunk trying to sleep, but she was not sympathetic.

'Oh shut up. You're trying to frighten me,' she'd say, 'Mum! Diane's trying to frighten me again. Tell her to stop!'

And I'd get a scolding because poor Debbie was easy to frighten.

But of all the presences in the flat, the scariest was the one known as Daddy. Absent most of the day, this apparition would erupt without warning through the front door long after I'd gone to bed – huge and bulky, black hair awry, dark eyes flashing, hands as big as shovels, with a strange sour smell wafting around him like an aura and a voice like a lion's roar. And then the shouting would start.

Debbie would cower in her bed too scared to move, listening to the arguments raging outside which were often punctuated by the sound of blows and my mother's sobbing. We'd long for it all to stop, but when it did the silence was almost worse. What had happened to Mum? Was she hurt? Was she even alive? We were too paralysed by fear to go and look.

Yet the next morning there she was, bright and smiling, crisp in her freshly-ironed shirt and jeans, briskly cooking breakfast as if nothing had happened. If it wasn't for the occasional new bruise under her eye you'd never know the events of the night before were anything more than a bad dream.

Any small child would have been disturbed by such an atmosphere, I suppose, but I seemed to react in a way that at times appeared to Mum to be almost deranged. One day, for example, for no reason at all I seemed to take violently against the teapot. A sturdy affair of white china, the teapot had sat blamelessly beside the stove every single day of my life and I'd watched it make countless cups of tea without objection. But now for some reason the very sight of it made me almost hysterical. Every time Mum went near it I shouted, 'No! No! Don't touch!' and grabbed her skirt and tried to drag her away. I was only a tiny tot of three years old but the sudden strength in my little fingers and the vehemence of my protests were positively alarming.

Mum unhooked me as best she could but it was very difficult for her to get on with her chores. I hung about the kitchen all day long, getting in the way, clinging onto her leg and screaming and crying whenever she approached the teapot. By evening she'd had enough; and when I threw another tantrum even more aggressive than the last as she brushed against the teapot on her way to fill a hot water bottle from the kettle, she picked me up and put me firmly to bed.

But early the next morning there was a sudden thud and a scream and I ran out to the kitchen to find the teapot smashed on the floor and Mum writhing in pain with the most enormous blisters I've ever seen popping up all over her legs.

'Daddy done it!' I said, bursting into tears.

'No. No, it was an accident . . .' Mum gasped as she staggered off to casualty with our lovely neighbour Glenys Stone. But I knew the truth, and years later Mum admitted it. My father wasn't pleased with the way she'd cooked his breakfast so he snatched up the teapot, full of freshly-brewed tea, and hurled it at her.

Mum was too stressed coping with her injuries, looking after the family and covering up the truth in front of the district nurse, who called in every day to change her dressings, to ponder the odd coincidence. Whatever made me pick that particular time to take against the teapot?

And this wasn't the first time I'd made a fuss in advance. A year or so before, Mum's friend Brenda popped in for a cup of tea and, being a kindly soul who loved small children, she wanted to sit cute little me on her knee. Normally I was happy to have a cuddle with Brenda but that day, the moment Mum popped Brenda's cup down in front of her on the table, I got a bad attack of the fidgets. I slithered and wriggled and kept trying to climb off Brenda's knee and the more I struggled to get down the more determined she became to hang on to me. I became greatly agitated and slipped around so much that Mum got cross.

'Diane, sit still will you!' she said sharply, and at that exact moment Brenda leaned forward to pick up her cup and it slid through her fingers and burning tea spilled over my arm. 'Oh no!' cried Brenda in distress, 'Look what she's done with her jerking around!'

But in fact I'd been sitting quite still listening to Mum at that point. She hadn't burned me because I was wriggling to get down, I was wriggling to get down because I knew she was going to burn me. I've got the scars to this day.

Poor Mum. It was just one thing after another. To make matters worse, my father, who'd recently come out of the army, was trying to set up an electrical repair business and lack of progress coupled with shortage of cash was making him increasingly stressed. Day after day he walked the streets of Swansea pushing flyers through doors advertising his services, and at night he'd come home and vent his frustrations on Mum. And as the discord in the flat increased, so did my strange behaviour.

I can only assume now that my unseen protectors moved in closer to support me as the situation at home deteriorated, but at the time I only knew that the flat became even more spooky.

One afternoon my grandfather, my father's father who ran a business in Kenya, happened to be visiting Wales and he popped in. Eager to show off as ever, I dashed into the lounge to fetch some toy I'd wanted him to see. It was lying on the settee but as I skipped towards it, hand outstretched, the room seemed to change. The air in front of me quivered, colours streamed before my eyes and out of nowhere a man materialised. Tall and dark with pleated, sandy-beige trousers, a leather belt and light shirt, there was nothing ethereal or other-worldly about him. His figure was not transparent or wispy. He looked as real and solid as my brother Gary, who I'd passed in the hall seconds before. In fact, if I hadn't witnessed his abrupt arrival I'd have thought he was someone come to see my father about work.

The strange man smiled at me with what was probably intended to be a nice smile. 'Hello,' he said gently, in a foreign-sounding voice that was weirdly familiar.

I was completely horrified. I couldn't take my eyes off

his face. It was brown and leathery and scored and grooved with dozens and dozens of deep lines. It was a jigsaw puzzle of a face and I knew just where I'd seen it before. It was the Lined Man come out from the shadows of the night. I'd never seen him in broad daylight before and in the harsh glare of the sun his face, to me, was even more ghastly than I'd realised. I'd never seen anything like it and I was totally appalled. Shocked to the very soles of my feet, I somehow stumbled out of the room. I don't remember any more until hours later.

Apparently I staggered into the kitchen in what appeared to be some sort of trance. I was stiff as a board, my eyes were dilated and I made no response to any questions. I was impervious to pleas, shakings or hugs, and my terrified mum could only conclude that I'd suffered a convulsion. Fortunately my grandfather was a quick-thinking man and he'd come across all sorts of odd medical emergencies in Africa. Taking in the situation at a glance he scooped me up like a little white statue, put me in his big car and raced me to hospital.

The doctors were just as baffled as everyone else. I was kept in for several days while tests for meningitis and fluid on the brain were carried out. Every test came back negative and I was soon my normal perky self again, though raving about some strange hallucination I'd had. In the end they decided I must have suffered a fit. They prescribed phenobarbitol to help me sleep and advised Mum to keep me calm at all times.

This was easier said than done. Back home I refused to be left alone for a minute, would not enter an empty room without an escort and hated going to bed because no amount of tranquil routine during the day seemed able to prevent the 'nightmares' that plagued my sleep.

I realised that the man with the funny voice who spoke to me, and the man with the horribly lined face I'd seen in the lounge were one and the same person. And now that he'd appeared to me in full, he seemed to think there was no longer any need to keep his face hidden when he came to my room for a chat. Night after night as I lay in bed trying to sleep I'd hear his voice, open my eyes and there he would be, a dark shape sitting in the corner of the room, his awful face clear, even though in shadow.

'It's all right, don't worry,' he'd whisper. 'Don't be alarmed. I'll look after you. I'm keeping you safe.'

But I didn't feel safe. Screaming in horror I'd leap out of bed and rush off to find Mum. And Mum, for her part terrified that in my hysterical state I'd overheat my brain and have another convulsion, would carry me into the kitchen where she'd wring out a cloth in the sink to make a cool compress, sit me on her knee, put the flannel on my head and rock me back and forth, back and forth, stroking my tense shoulders and calming me with soothing words.

Yet even on her lap it wasn't always safe. 'Look, there's another man over there!' I'd suddenly shout. Or, 'There's a man looking in the window!' And since we were on the fourth floor it's no wonder she didn't believe me.

'No, no, it's just a dream,' Mum would chant softly,

'just a dream. Now how about a story? Once upon a time there were three bears . . .'

And that's how Dad invariably found us when he stormed in drunk. He'd blunder into the kitchen working himself up for a row and then stop short. There was something about the sight of me sitting there peering out at him from beneath a large pink flannel that seemed to make him pause and change direction.

'Huh!' he'd snort in disgust, flinging down his keys. 'Huh!', then he'd stomp away. A few minutes later we'd hear loud snores coming from the bedroom and I knew with complete certainty that it was suddenly quite all right to go back to bed.

Was it an accident, I wonder now, that my nightmares so often coincided with the nights my father came home more than usually drunk and aggressive? Or could the Lined Man have been scaring me on purpose in order to protect both me and my mother?

Back then, of course, such an idea never entered my head. All I knew was that this peculiar stranger frightened me. I couldn't understand why no one else could see him or why he wouldn't leave me alone. Nothing I could do or say would get rid of him. But it didn't stop me trying.

One night shortly after putting me to bed, Mum came back with Debbie who, being 18 months older, was allowed to stay up a little later, but when she tried to open the door, it wouldn't budge. She pushed and pushed but the door seemed to hit some sort of obstruction and spring back.

'Diane, what have you done with this door?' cried Mum, banging on the paintwork that she kept so scrupulously clean. 'Come on. Open it at once.'

There was a muffled reply that she couldn't make out but the door stayed firmly shut. In the end, with the aid of my brothers, she was able to force her way into my room. As the door burst open there was a thud, and two mattresses half swathed in sheets fell to the floor in the doorway. There I was inside, sitting calmly on my bare bed frame, beneath Debbie's bed which had also been stripped. Ingenious – in my own way – as my father, I'd decided to keep the Lined Man out of my room by barricading the door with mattresses. But of course I might have known, there was no way he could be discouraged by a few wire springs and a bit of fabric . . .

Chapter Two

I was flying. The night sky, blazing ice-blue with stars, was wrapped around me, a gentle breeze lifted my hair and miles and miles below I could see the lights of a city strung out orange and yellow across the darkness.

The Lined Man was somewhere close, but for once I was too entranced to care. Now that I was nearly six I was getting more used to him, and though he still startled me if he appeared suddenly, I realised that he never did me any harm. There was no need to be frightened.

'I want to show you something,' he'd said and then somehow I wasn't in my bed any more but flying down the stairs, out through the door and away over the rooftops.

'Where are we going?' I gasped when I'd got used to the breathless, soaring feeling.

'Africa,' he replied.

Then the cool air became warm on my face, the sky lightened and I was looking down on a vast baked-biscuit landscape splashed with green, and way off in the distance I could see a sparkling sea far bluer than Swansea Bay had ever been, even on the balmiest summer day.

'Look!' said the Lined Man and as I looked we seemed to swoop in closer. Mint-humbug zebra stood knee-deep in tawny grass, giraffe browsed amongst strange flat-topped trees and far away against the horizon a group of elephants was strolling. Then the land became more lush, buildings cruised into view and I glimpsed a house. Oranges peeped from the branches of trees in the garden and through the windows I could see beds all draped in gauzy white. Most fascinating of all, creeping over the ground below I could see dozens of giant black beetles. The biggest beetles I'd ever seen.

'That's Africa,' said the Lined Man.

'Africa!' I thought in amazement and then, heaven knows why when it was all so exciting, I seemed to fall back to sleep.

*   *   *

'Mum,' I said the next morning as I was eating my corn-flakes from the Tupperware bowl she'd recently bought, 'I flew down the stairs last night.'

'She's telling lies again,' said Debbie, ladling sugar into her own Tupperware bowl. Hers was yellow, mine pink and Gary's green. Mum liked going to Tupperware parties; it got her out of the house, away from Dad.

'She's not telling lies,' said Mum. 'She was dreaming. It was a dream, Diane.'

'No, it wasn't a dream. I really flew. I flew down the stairs and out into the sky.'

'In your mind you did,' Mum said, squirting washing-up liquid into the bowl.

'No, I can fly. Really.'

'No you can't,' Debbie said. 'If you can fly then go on – why don't you fly out of the window now and show us.'

''Cos I'm eating my cornflakes.'

'See – you know you can't. Liar! Liar!'

'You two! That's enough.' Mum banged down the washing-up liquid. 'Anyway, I've got something exciting to tell you. Guess where we're going.'

'The fair?' suggested Debbie.

'No, better than the fair. We're going on holiday. To Africa! We're going to see Daddy's family.'

I sucked cornflakes off my spoon. 'I've been to Africa,' I said.

'No you haven't,' said Debbie.

'I have. I flew.'

Mum sighed. Deeply.

But incredibly, considering neither Debbie nor I could remember ever leaving Wales before, we really were going to Africa for Christmas. (Though poor Gary, who was doing important things at school had to stay behind with friends. He could go in the long summer holidays, he was promised.) My wealthy grandfather had taken quite a shine to us on his visit to Swansea, it seemed, and now he was treating us to this trip of a lifetime. Mum dashed about for weeks in a flurry of preparations. Our flimsiest summer clothes were inspected and then rejected. New shoes were pur-chased, along with two smart lime green and navy dresses and other finery, and for days on end the kitchen hummed with endless washing and ironing. Suitcases were packed and repacked and Debbie had to have her waist-length hair cut short.

'It'll be much too hot out there,' Mum said, critically fingering Debbie's trailing locks and lifting them up off her neck to show how cool it would be without them. But Debbie howled.

'I'll look like a boy!' she wept, but her lovely long brown tresses were snipped to the floor all the same.

She was still crying when we went to bed that night. Slightly guilty that my own shoulder-length tangles had just about scraped into the approved category and escaped the scissors (either that or Mum couldn't face my inevitable tantrums), I climbed up into Debbie's bunk to give her a comforting hug.

'You don't look like a boy. You're still beautiful Debbie. Really,' I assured her, but Debbie continued to sniff. 'Your hair will grow back and anyway you'll love Africa. You'll see zebras and elephants and giraffes and – and your bed won't be like this, it'll have net curtains . . .'

Debbie struggled free from my arms.

'How d'you know what it'll have? You don't know what's there.'

'I do,' I said, 'I've been.'

Debbie snorted and wrenched away, turning her face crossly to the wall. 'Liar,' she said and she pulled the covers right up over her head.

I never gave up though.

It was a very, very long way to Kenya. We were such an age on the plane that they gave us pillows and blankets and reclined our seats and told us to go to sleep. But I still couldn't help myself.

'. . . and as well as lions,' I whispered to Debbie, as she snuggled down with her teddy, 'there are these great big black beetles . . .'

'Yuk!' Debbie gave a muted scream, 'Shut up! Why are you telling me about beetles? You know I hate creepy crawlies. Shut up! There aren't any beetles.'

'Don't worry,' I said, 'I'll look after you.'

But for some reason Debbie wasn't comforted.

Eventually, after what seemed like days, the blankets and pillows were put away, my father finished his drink and Mum dressed Debbie and me in our matching lime green and navy outfits. She patted her hair back into place, reapplied her lipstick and then the wheels of our plane were whizzing thrillingly along the runway at Nairobi airport and our grandfather was waiting in his big, navy blue Mercedes.

When we stepped from the plane it was like walking in front of the oven when Mum was taking a cake out. There was a brilliant blue sky so bright it hurt our eyes and the heat warmed me right down to my toes. I loved it. Exotic greenery crowded close to the terminus building, laughing people with glossy brown skin tossed our suitcases onto trolleys and the air smelled warm and foreign. Out of the corner of my eye I saw a huge black beetle scuttle across the ground. I was about to point it out to Debbie but I thought better of it.

My grandfather turned out to live in a big white house with a verandah running round the outside and cool shady rooms indoors. Vibrant purple bougainvillea scrambled over the garden walls and shiny dark citrus trees grew around the tough green elephant grass.

My grandfather had his own business installing cameras into cinemas, my mother told us, and he seemed to be very rich because smiling servants with white aprons and bare feet padded softly around the house doing all the work. My mother didn't have to make so much as a cup of tea.

Chief of the servants was Ramazani, a thin, dark little man with white teeth all bunched up in the front of his mouth and a big gold ring on his finger of which he was immensely proud. My grandfather had given him the ring years before and Ramazani was eternally grateful. We saw a lot of Ramazani because he seemed to have been entrusted with the care of Debbie and me while the grown-ups went out to smart parties and functions.

'Now come along Little Ladies,' he'd say, 'You've got to be good tonight.' And then he'd let us do whatever we wanted. We raided the fridge for unlimited cold colas, picked oranges off the trees and ran in and out of the little two-roomed cottage in the garden, where Ramazani lived with his family, as if it was our own. Ramazani's grandchildren, Tony and his little sister Tulie, used to stare at us with enormous brown eyes as if they'd never seen anything like it. I don't suppose they had.

They invited me over for tea one day. My grandfather didn't think it was right that I should eat with the servants but Aunt Trixie, who lived with him, said: 'Oh, let her go.' So I did.

There was no table in Ramazani's house, just a concrete floor spread with leaves and a few rugs. Ramazani's wife ladled sweet potatoes and cabbage onto even bigger leaves and put them on the floor in front of us and then we all leaned forward and scooped the food up with our hands – something Mum never allowed us to do at home. It was brilliant.

Most days we were allowed to go out with Ramazani. Tony was teaching Debbie and me to talk in Swahili and we learned to count, and between lessons Ramazani took us up the road to the dusty little shack that served as the local shop. It was run by a very, very old man who walked with a stick because he only had one leg and he was helped by a little boy who had a strange milky white eye that didn't look at you.

The best bit of the shop, as far as we were concerned, was the shelf on which stood two huge glass jars crammed with yellow sweets rather like giant pineapple chunks. The old man used to dispense these candies singly and every day he'd creakily lift down the jar for us, unscrew the lid with slow, arthritic fingers and carefully extract two precious chunks. Debbie and I thought it was the most wonderful shop we'd ever come across.

As Christmas approached we begged some money from our grandfather, dashed up to the shop and told the old man that we didn't want one or two sweets as usual, we'd like all of them, both whole jars. The poor old man was completely taken aback. He'd never sold so much in one go before and had never handled such a big note. He had no change to give us but we didn't care. We didn't want change. We gladly swapped the money for the two enormous jars and, hugging one each, we struggled back to present them to Tony and Tulie. To our surprise, instead of looking happy, the brother and sister started to cry. They were quite overcome to receive such a lavish gift.

For a moment or two it was as if they couldn't comprehend that the entire contents of the jars was for them. Then suddenly Tony seemed to understand. He dashed away a tear with the back of his hand, seized one of the jars and started excitedly scrabbling at the lid.

'Wait, wait, children,' said Ramazani stepping in. He removed the glass from Tony's eager fingers, 'Patience. Make them last. Just one a day.' Then he unscrewed the lid, offered Debbie and me first choice and finally selected two golden candies for his grandchildren. 'Now say thank you to the Little Ladies.'

Back home some of the children we knew might have yelled and protested to be so swiftly parted from their new gift, but Tony just smiled. 'Thank you Little Ladies,' he said, cheek bulging, and turned to help Tulie who was having difficulty getting the big sticky cube into her small mouth.

Debbie and I were just delighted that our gift was such a success.

We were having a wonderful time in Africa. Sometimes our grandfather would load us into the blue Mercedes and drive us out to the bush to look at wild animals. I'd seen them before, of course, on my nocturnal visit, but it was even better to get a close up view. And boy did my grandfather like to get close up. I think he must have been a bit of a daredevil because he'd edge his car so close to the elephants you could clearly see the whites of their eyes. Once he overdid it and a big old bull with chipped yellowish tusks trumpeted angrily and turned and chased us up the road. My grandfather put his foot down to the floor and roared us away in a cloud of dust, laughing in delight.

Once we even stayed the night in the bush, sleeping in a round mud hut with a thatched roof and lions growling right outside the door.

Another time my grandfather took us to a huge lake, rosy with flamingoes as far as the eye could see. Something must have startled them because suddenly, for no reason at all, they lifted up into the air, thousands and thousands of them, and flew across the sky, a giant pink banner against the blue – only to wheel round and water-ski back into the lake again.

Then there was a trip to the coastal town of Mombasa, where slender palm trees leaned out towards the waves and lithe brown men shinned up them like clever monkeys, gripping the trunks with their legs, to throw down coconuts into waiting baskets below.

'Can I have a go? Can I have a go?' I begged.

And laughing kindly, the men stood aside and helped

me to ascend the smooth grey trunks – which was not quite as easy as they made it look.

Further along the shore were fabulous beaches with sands of pure, pure white, so bright it dazzled your eyes. When we first saw them, Debbie and I tossed off our shoes and went whooping down towards the sea, but we'd only gone a few yards when Debbie shrieked in horror and stopped. I slowed and looked back.

'There are crabs!' Debbie screamed in disgust.

And when I looked more closely I saw that the sand was covered with hundreds and hundreds of tiny white crustaceans. They didn't bother me, I simply dodged between them, but Debbie and my mother clung together at the top of the beach, shoes in hand, refusing to go any further.

Debbie had a bit of a phobia about crawling things. Just as I'd told her before we arrived, Kenya did seem to specialise in these enormous black beetles and when we ventured outside I was forever having to stamp clear a path for her to walk along or she wouldn't move. I didn't dare mention it again – even though an 'I told you so' leapt instantly to my lips from the first night when we were shown to beds swathed in gauzy drapes which weren't curtains but mosquito nets – but it was obvious to me that the Lined Man really had shown me Africa. All the things I'd predicted to Debbie before we left had been right in every detail. Yet, oddly enough, since we'd arrived in Kenya I hadn't actually seen the Lined Man, though I often sensed his presence. When I was watching the zebra, or listening to the frogs croaking in the night it was as if he was standing at my elbow, smiling with satisfaction. 'Look!' he seemed to say. 'Isn't it wonderful?' and it was.

The other amazing thing about Africa was the change in my father. A different man seemed to have stepped off the plane with us – a man on his very best behaviour. There was no shouting, my mother didn't cry and sometimes the two of them laughed. Sometimes, my father even put his arm round her. Occasionally, when my grandfather had visitors, I'd watch this handsome, stylishly dressed man moving amongst them with an easy smile and a lilting, charming voice and I wondered who he could be. Was he really related to me? I didn't seem to have met him before.

Yet improved as he was, there were times when my father couldn't quite slam the door on his inner viciousness. Now and then he simply couldn't help himself; he couldn't resist picking away at my mother. Mum had beautiful skin, literally like porcelain, but it was very, very delicate so she never ventured out without covering herself up and putting on a hat, and for some reason this fastidiousness irritated my father.

'Get some sun, woman!' he'd order impatiently. 'Look at you, you're pale as a ghost. Get in the sun.'

So one day Mum left her hat off and, of course, she was burned to a crisp in minutes.

The next morning my father viewed her painful scarlet burns with disgust. 'Look at the state of you,' he complained. 'You look like a beacon with your bright red nose.'

He also took exception to her clothes. Mum had very slim legs but she felt they were embarrassingly thin so she constantly covered them up with trousers.

'Why don't you wear feminine clothes like other women?' asked my father tetchily, when Mum appeared for an excursion in cool white slacks and a filmy blouse. 'Why can't you wear a skirt?'

So my mother put on a skirt and throughout lunch Dad made the other guests laugh with constant jokes about Mum's 'flamingo legs'.

'What's the matter with you, flamingo legs? Lost your sense of humour?' he sneered when Mum failed to smile quickly enough.

But these taunts were so trivial compared to Dad's usual outbursts and we were having such a good time that we scarcely noticed them.

One morning my grandfather brought the big blue Mercedes round to the front of the house and told Debbie and me to jump in.

'We're going somewhere different today,' he said.

'Will there be lions?' asked Debbie.

'No,' said Grandfather.

'Zebra?' I asked.

'No,' said Grandfather.

'Oh I know,' I said suddenly, 'there'll be a snake.'

My grandfather paused and gave me an odd, weighing up sort of look for a second. Then he said. 'No, no wildlife at all I don't suppose.'

Debbie and I, who were becoming a bit blasé now about the wonders of Africa, were a little disappointed. We were even more disappointed when Grandfather drove a little way out of town and then pulled up beside a railway track with not a wildebeest, flamingo or lion to be seen. We stared up and down the empty line. The long silver rails flashed in the sunshine and stretched off unremarkably as far as the eye could see. To our eyes one railway line looked very much like another, and this was no different to the track we'd seen in Swansea.

'Are we going to watch the trains?' asked Debbie politely.

'Possibly,' said Grandfather, 'but it's the line itself that's the interesting bit. That track was built by your great, great-grandfather who was called Ronald Owen Preston. And if it wasn't for that line, Nairobi probably wouldn't be here at all. When your great, great-grandfather arrived this place was just a marshy waterhole. They called it supply Depot 327.'

Looking at the streets, the leafy gardens and the cars sliding by, this was very difficult to imagine, but Grandfather said it was important we should know about our family history and he told us the story.

Apparently his grandfather, Ronald, had originally come from Liverpool and had gone to India to work as an engineer on the railways, and when the decision was made to build a railway right across Kenya from Mombasa to Lake Victoria, great, great-grandfather Preston came from India with a band of Indian construction workers to begin the task.

'Back then they nicknamed it the Lunatic Express,'

said Grandfather, 'because they said it was such an impossible job only a lunatic would attempt it.'

And it certainly seemed a crazy scheme. The men had to cross deserts and vast, sun-baked wildernesses; the workers were struck down with malaria, dysentery and terrible fevers; their pack animals were decimated by Tsetse fly and ferocious storms blew up and floods swept away the rails they'd just laid. Rhinos charged the construction gangs, termites ate the wooden sleepers, giraffes snatched washing off the lines, monkeys pulled down the tents and a band of strange, maneless lions began stalking the workers, dragging so many to their deaths under cover of darkness that the fearful crew believed the animals were possessed by the devil.

Yet despite all these problems the line was completed in 1901. 'And your great, great-grandmother laid the final rail at the water's edge in Lake Victoria,' said Grandfather. 'They named the town Florence, after her.' (Now Kisumu.)

Debbie was impressed. 'Fancy having a town named after you.'

But I was worried about all those animals driven from their homes by speeding trains.

'Didn't they mind having a train coming through?' I asked.

'If it wasn't for the train, most of the towns in Kenya wouldn't be here,' said Grandfather, 'they were built round the stations. Anyway, in a way the people might have known it was coming. They do say there was an ancient Maasai prophecy that one day an iron snake would crawl across their land.'

I stared at the line curving away to the horizon. If I half-closed my eyes and imagined I was looking at it from a very long way off, it did look a bit like a giant silvery snake.

'Oh yes – I see,' I said.

And Grandfather gave me that odd, considering look again. Then he seemed to remember something.

'Right,' he said, pulling open the door of the car, 'Now we're going to see my mother who's your great-grandmother.'

'Wow,' said Debbie. In her mind this lady must be really ancient.

Great-grandmother lived in a house similar to my grandfather's, only even larger. The big, dimly-lit rooms gleamed with dark wood, from the highly-polished parquet floors to the chunky sideboards twinkling with silver and the little ebony tables crammed with photographs and ornaments. Large whirly fans spun on the ceiling and stuffed animals with big teeth roared silently from the dark walls.

I didn't like those dead animals. Their cold glass eyes seemed to follow me round the room and one of them was the oddest beast – a faded khaki brute with a twisted mouth frozen into a snarl. A lion without a mane.

Great-grandmother was a strange creature. Once she'd been very beautiful, my mother told me, with a hint of Indian somewhere in her ancestry, but now she was extremely old and frail with a peculiarly white face and hands. When I peered close I could see that her skin was covered with a thick layer of ghostly powder.

I thought perhaps she had to be careful of sunburn like my mother, but much later the two of them had a disagreement, presumably along the lines that Mum wasn't good enough for the great Ronald Preston's great-grandson and, stung, I heard Mum fling back: 'Well at least I don't pretend to be something I'm not.' And I realised Mum thought that Great Grandmother was putting on airs and graces and trying to pretend she was much more refined than she really was.

But if Great-grandmother didn't take much to Mum she certainly held no grudges against me.

Debbie and I were lined up for her inspection and although she seemed to approve of Debbie she kept coming back to me. She turned my face this way and that in her floury little paw, looked deep into my eyes and then patted my head.

'You're the one,' she said with a satisfied smile. 'You're the special one.'

I was flattered of course, but baffled. What did she mean 'special'? Was it because I was the youngest perhaps? Or the naughtiest? Maybe being so small for my age I was the cutest?

'Come on,' said Great-grandmother taking my hand. 'Come and see.'

And she took me across the room to show me one of her ornaments, a fat little bald headed man with a radiant smile and a big pot belly.

'Rub his belly,' she said encouragingly. 'This is Buddha. And you are the special one. You will take things on.'

I had no idea what she was talking about but I liked the jolly little man and after that, whenever I visited, we always went to say hello to him together.

It was only years afterwards that I discovered that as well as being a renowned railway engineer my great, great-grandfather in later life had an even more unusual skill. The local tribesmen believed that he was a healer and they took their sick to him to be cured. At one stage he opened a shop and for years gave readings and conducted a healing clinic from there.

But that was for the future. At the time I thought little of Great-grandmother's odd words. Old people said funny things sometimes. Christmas was approaching and Debbie and I were swept along in the excitement. We were even dressed in our finest clothes and taken as a treat to dinner in a grand hotel with some of Grand-father's friends. The women wore long dresses and glittered with jewels and the table was laden with caviar and the finest champagne. But it was wasted on us. Debbie and I much preferred Coca-cola and fish fingers.

On Christmas Eve the adults went out to yet another party and Debbie and I were sent to bed to make Christmas morning come more quickly. We couldn't sleep, of course, so when we were sure the coast was clear we crept out to the drawing room to see if there were any presents for us. A traditional tree complete with fairy lights had been arranged in the corner and beneath the tree was a satisfying heap of brightly wrapped parcels. Although we hadn't realised it at the time, Mum must have brought a whole suitcase full of Christmas gifts with her from Wales to make sure we didn't miss out.

Highly delighted, we checked the labels of the gifts on the top and gave a few choice items a quick squeeze to see if we could guess what was inside. As I held one beautiful parcel in my hands a sudden picture of our favourite TV programme, *Tom and Jerry*, flashed into my head. Cartoon cat Tom was chasing the naughty mouse Jerry through the TV-family living room and it seemed completely obvious to me that the toy beneath my fingers was connected to this scene.

'It's a Tom and a Jerry!' I said, hugging the parcel to my chest, 'You've got one too.'

'How can you tell?' said Debbie scornfully. 'Be careful. Don't tear the paper or they'll know. Come on, we'd better get back before someone comes.'

Reluctantly I replaced my Tom and Jerry toys – I knew they were a Tom and Jerry – and we skipped back to bed and snuggled down to await morning. Neither of us thought we could possibly sleep, but of course we did.

At some point in the night I woke suddenly, as if someone had shaken me. The room was pitch black, Debbie was lying still, her breathing soft and regular, and outside the crickets and the bull frogs were making their usual nocturnal song – yet something was wrong. I sensed eyes looking at me in the darkness and turning my head I saw the Lined Man standing by the bed. I jumped. It had been so long now since I'd seen him that I'd almost forgotten those troubled nights in Wales.

'Ssshhhh,' he said, putting his finger to his lips, 'Don't be scared. It's going to be all right. I'm taking care of you.'

He was going to protect me, which was good – but why did I need protecting? Everything seemed completely normal. Before I could ask what he meant, there was a noise in the corridor. A door gently closed, quiet footsteps came down the hall and then the bedroom door slowly swung open. I glanced back at the Lined Man but he'd vanished, and now there was someone else creeping into the room. An overpowering smell of whisky – I knew it was whisky because my grandfather had a bottle he poured from almost every night – wafted through the mosquito nets. Then the curtains around Debbie's bed parted and my grandfather was standing there.

'Girls, are you okay?' he whispered, his voice strangely thick and blurred, 'Are you okay girls? I'm just going to climb into bed with you. Don't be afraid.' And he pulled back the covers.

Utter horror shot through me, though I couldn't tell why. I didn't know what he was going to do but I knew this wasn't nice. This wasn't right. Small as I was I jumped straight out of bed and confronted him.

'You'd better get out, now!' I said loudly.

My grandfather looked nervously towards the door. I could smell cigar smoke on his breath mingled with the whisky. He went to put his arm round my shoulders but I stepped back quickly. 'Don't be afraid dear . . . don't be . . .'

'Get out, now!' I said again, my voice rising.

Grandfather straightened up. 'Good. Well . . . As long as you girls are okay . . .' And he stumbled off towards the door. I watched him go and I stood there listening until the sound of his hurrying feet had faded into silence.

Debbie stirred. 'Was someone there . . . not Father Christmas was it?'

'No . . . not Father Christmas . . .' I said climbing back into bed. 'Someone quite different . . .'

I couldn't look my grandfather in the face for the rest of our visit and he seemed to avoid me too. Africa was still wonderful. I still loved it but I realised that it wasn't quite the total paradise I'd first thought.

Chapter Three

What was wrong with my father? Why did he have to behave the way he did? It was a subject that puzzled me from a very early age. I used to sit there and look at him and think, 'Just what *is* the matter with you! What's going on? Why do you do it?'

I don't remember him ever showing any of us any affection or love. Quite the opposite. Even when he wasn't shouting and screaming at us he couldn't seem to help being nasty. If Debbie was passing by his chair he always had to stick his foot out to trip her up. If Gary accidentally walked in front of the TV, my father just had to clip him round the head.

Once Gary went on an errand to the corner shop but forgot Mum's cigarettes. My father sent him back for the cigarettes plus a pint of milk. When Gary returned with those my father sent him off again for a bag of sugar. When he got back with the sugar he had to go off again for matches and so on until Gary was pouring with sweat and his eyes full of tears.

My father never read us a bedtime story, never kicked a football with the boys or taught us to ride our bikes. The only concessions he ever made to family life were the very rare occasions when he took us out for a family barbecue to a local country park – and that was probably because if he hadn't, he'd never have used his precious new barbecue at all. Even then we always had to play the game my father himself devised – hunt the matchbox. And Debbie's matchbox was always the one with a spider in it instead of the promised 50p piece because – as well he knew – Debbie was terrified of creepy crawlies. Her anguished scream as she gingerly opened the box and then dropped it in horror, made his day.

Once we were walking to school and my father sailed by in his brand new blue Jag, windows down, Elvis Presley's 'In the Ghetto' blasting the whole street. As he saw us he waved and pulled into the kerb a little way ahead. Astonished, yet ever hopeful that Dad would one day miraculously morph into the father we'd like him to be, we ran up to the car, but just as we were reaching for the door handle, he accelerated away, drove on another hundred yards and stopped again.

Breathlessly we set off once more, but just as we reached him he drove off again. Three times we chased him down the road and three times he drove off before we could open the door. Then, clearly bored with the game, he roared away into the distance, beeping the horn, laughing his head off and shouting over his shoulder, 'The exercise'll do you good.'

Yet we didn't bother complaining, even to each other. These were my father's light-hearted moments and we were almost grateful for them. Mostly he was in a much darker mood. Meal times were particularly tense and fraught with danger. My father didn't eat with us. He sat alone in the living room with a tray on his knee while the rest of us gathered round the kitchen table. But although he was out of sight, his sharp ears must have been constantly straining to catch every sound and he controlled us from a distance. Laughing was strictly forbidden – anyone who laughed was immediately sent to bed. As was anyone who coughed. Even talking was frowned upon. We were expected to finish our meals quickly and in silence.

Unfortunately the rules made us so nervous the slightest thing would bring on a fit of the giggles and the more Mum begged us to be quiet the more we couldn't help exploding. Many a time we all ended up in bed without any supper and it was always me, being the smallest, who was sent downstairs when the coast was clear to grab a handful of cereal from the pantry to bring back to my starving siblings. Once I grabbed the whole packet of cornflakes, tipped a tin of sticky condensed milk straight into the box and raced it upstairs where the four of us devoured the lot with our fingers.

My father was very particular about his food. He had to have three courses for dinner, it had to be ready when he arrived home and it had to be perfect in every detail. One evening he thought he detected a little mud on the lettuce Mum was about to serve him, just as she was grinding the black pepper over it for him.

'What have you done woman?' he screamed angrily,

as if he'd just discovered he'd been given cyanide, 'You haven't done the lettuce properly!' and he yanked the plate off the tray and threw it all over the carpet.

'Fetch me another one!' he ordered as Mum crawled around the floor on her hands and knees gathering discarded leaves and up she had to get to rush off to make more salad.

On other occasions he insisted on a full cooked breakfast before work, so Mum had to get up at 6 am to prepare it. She'd spend ages scurrying around the kitchen getting everything just so and then he'd take one look at his plate, declare the sausage was burned or the egg overdone and throw the whole lot out of the window. As we were living on the fourth floor at the time this made quite a mess, but he did it so often the skinny old Alsatian up the road took to hanging around the dustbins beneath our flat to await breakfast from heaven. He must have thought it rained bacon and eggs in that magical spot.

Even when my father wasn't around, his malevolent presence seemed to hang over us, taking the edge off any fun we managed to scrape together for ourselves.

In the way that childhood summers do, those far off days of the long school holidays always seemed to be especially glorious and whenever the sun shone, Mum, Auntie Kathleen and various friends and neighbours from the flats would gather up us children and set off for a day at the beach.

Mum used to whisper to us about it the night before, as she tucked us into bed, filling us with excitement and anticipation. Next morning we'd be up ridiculously early, creeping around so as not to wake father and make him angry, yet silently willing him to open his eyes, get up and leave for work. He couldn't go quickly enough for our liking. Then, the minute the door slammed behind him we'd spring into joyous life. Everyone dashed into the tiny kitchen to make the picnic. Mum feverishly buttered great stacks of bread and the four of us children would spread them with jam or meat paste. Into the bag would go slices of home-made cake, rosy apples and anything else Mum could find. Swimsuits were rolled into towels, buckets and spades pulled out of cupboards and then, arms bulging, we'd burst out into the street to make for the bus stop.

By the time the big red bus rolled up there were so many of us we'd practically fill it. Cousin Peter, five years older than me and already handsome with his curly blond hair, blue eyes and crisp white T-shirt was always the perfect gentleman and instantly offered his seat to any elderly lady who happened to get on. I was dragged onto Mum's lap, Debbie and the boys squeezed onto one seat together and chattering loudly we lurched off towards the seafront, pausing only to change buses halfway.

We thought the beach was wonderful, but in fact being so close to Swansea docks it must have reeked. There were great swathes of thick sludgy gloop which was probably a slurry of tar, oil and sand all mixed together. We called it 'Black Custard' and while the mums picked their way carefully to a patch of smooth, clean gold to spread out the towel encampment, we children ran to jump in the custard, roll around in it and come back encrusted in smelly grey from head to toe. Naturally our mothers refused to hand out sandwiches to children in that condition, so we'd be sent back to the water's edge – a very long way if the tide was out – to wash it all off again.

After lunch Peter would help us build the most fabulous sandcastle in Wales. He was quite a craftsman and a complete perfectionist even then. Debbie and I would run backwards and forwards fetching buckets of fresh sand while Peter, aided by Gary, smoothed our lumpy efforts and carefully shaped turrets, staircases and battlements. Then Peter would find a matchstick and cut little gothic windows and doors, add a flag made out of a lolly wrapper and stick and we'd end up with such an impressive building that the holiday-makers would stop and take photographs of it.

Yet, despite all the hours he'd spent on the castle, at the end of the day, before we went home, Peter always let us jump on it.

I had a bit of an obsession with digging as well as sandcastles back then, so when we tired of construction Peter used to help me excavate a huge hole. Then he'd put a fold-up chair inside it, get me to sit in it and would bury me up to my neck. I loved it.

The hours flew past at the beach but there always came a point halfway through the afternoon when a certain tension would start to build around the towel camp. Mum would keep looking at her watch. Then she'd start clearing away the sandwich wrappers and debris. Children would be called back from the distant waves. Peter was despatched to fetch buckets of water for foot washing and slowly we were re-buckled into our socks and shoes for the journey home.

As we scurried over the stone bridge back into town, Mum's anxiety increased. She fretted if the bus was late, worried if we were stuck in traffic and by the time we finally arrived at the flats she was quite agitated. We all knew why. My father had to have his dinner ready on time. If it wasn't, there'd be trouble.

'Would you like me to come in with you, Auntie Pat?' Peter would offer bravely.

But Mum always refused. 'Oh no, don't be daft,' she'd say, 'I'll be okay.'

Only she wasn't okay. Nine times out of ten my father, with that awful sixth sense he seemed to possess, would choose that particular day to arrive home a little early and as soon as the door opened there he was ranting and raving.

'Where have you been? Do you know what the time is?' he'd shout, 'There's no dinner. Come on woman! Get to it!' and as she tried to pass him to get into the kitchen he'd give her a slap or a punch – just as he did to Gary when he walked in front of the TV. We hated to see him do that but we were quite powerless to stop him and it happened so often that it hardly registered as unusual. We just accepted that this was how some men treated their wives and Mum had been unlucky to annoy him.

Once, after rapidly peeling some potatoes and getting

them on to boil, Mum turned and noticed that we'd walked some sand into the hall. She dashed out with the dustpan and brush to sweep away the evidence before my father saw, but he caught her bending over the gleaming floor and gave her a vicious kick up the backside. Me, Gary and Debbie saw him do it but none of us dared protest. He'd turn on us if we did, which was the one thing Mum feared most. She always put on a brave face and made light of any pain she must be feeling because she didn't want us to worry, or do anything that would turn his anger in our direction. It was the only way for her to cope I suppose, but for a long time it made us feel as if this was normal life. As if she was to blame for my father's outbursts because of her carelessness. We couldn't acknowledge our feelings of anger, fear and injustice either to Mum or each other, so without realising it, the four of us must have buried them deep inside.

Looking back, with all this going on at home it wouldn't have been surprising if I'd been a bit disturbed, and perhaps I was. I often wet the bed, there was a permanent twisted feeling in the pit of my stomach that I was so used to I thought it was normal, and I followed Mum around like a little shadow.

When the day came that I had to go to school for the first time and leave her for a whole day, I was appalled. Mum tried to prepare me for the big day. 'You're going to school tomorrow just like Debbie. Instead of dropping Debbie off at the door like we normally do, you'll be going in with her! Won't that be fun?'

'No!' I screamed, 'I don't want to go. I want to stay at home with you.'

'You'll make lots of new friends,' Mum continued brightly, 'and you can wear your new red-and-white-checked dress with your white shoes and I've got you a new ribbon for your hair.'

But the lovely clothes didn't mollify me. I wouldn't even smile when Mum stitched little red bows around my white ankle socks to make them as pretty as my dress. I hardly slept the whole night and when I did finally drop off I wet the bed again.

Yet there was no getting out of it. The next morning I was dressed in my finery and dragged up the road with Debbie and all the other children. Mum held my hand very firmly and walked me right up to the classroom to meet the teacher. But I took one look at the dozens of little faces clustered around the tiny tables and screamed the place down. To my eyes the place seemed horribly crowded, because as well as the living children, I could see another lot of strangely vibrant kids mingling amongst them and some of these odd kids were waving at me. Yet no-one else took any notice of them. I knew there was something different about the ignored pupils but it was only later that I realised they were spirit children.

Even more troubling was that fact that one little girl, whose name was Lilly, had another absolutely identical girl almost attached to her arm. There was Lilly, a sturdy little thing with neat bobbed hair and a white pinafore dress, large as life and gaping at me worriedly, and right beside her stood a replica Lilly dressed in exactly the same clothes.

'You've got somebody following you!' I told her. 'Look! She's right there and she looks just like you!'

Lilly glanced round with a bewildered expresssion on her face and obviously saw no-one.

'She's there!' I cried in frustration. 'Look! She's got the same dress as you.'

Lilly backed away and then she started to cry, which only confused me more. Even though I was used to seeing the Lined Man I still wasn't accustomed to other invisible people appearing without warning and I couldn't understand what was going on or who this other girl was.

More alarmed than ever, I turned round to find Mum, but she, obviously assuming I was happily making friends, had taken the opportunity to slip quietly away. I ran to the window and was just in time to see her trim figure in her fitted black jacket and jeans hurrying off down the road. It was raining, the wind was coming in gusts and Mum's umbrella turned inside out as she struggled away down the hill.

'Mum!' I wailed, banging on the glass. But it was too late. She'd gone.

I spent the rest of the day clinging to the window, watching the raindrops sliding down the pane and waiting for Mum to come back. Wisely, though she came and talked kindly to me now and then, the teacher left me to it.

School did get better after that. Gradually I learned to

accept that I couldn't stay with Mum all the time and I began to enjoy the cheerful days with my classmates. Having brothers and a sister already I was quite used to the company of other children and I made friends quickly. Lilly never did get used to me though. She gave me a wide berth, as I did her. Small children find it easy to believe in monsters and fairies and invisible beings, so it wasn't difficult for me to conclude that the replica Lilly was some sort of other-worldly creature that no one else could see. From Lilly's reaction it was clear that I was the only one who could see her, but even this didn't seem particularly odd. It was quite plain to me, even then, that not everybody shared the same attributes. Some children had asthma, some did not; some wore glasses, some didn't; some could run really fast or sing beautifully while others couldn't. We all had different skills and mine seemed to be having the sort of eyes that could notice people that others didn't see. Even so it was sometimes unnerving to turn quickly and see double Lillies everywhere I went. I can only think now that Lilly must have had a twin sister who died at birth, but at the time I just reckoned that Lilly was a bit odd; a bit unlike the other children. I suspect the feeling was mutual.

Chapter Four

We were going up in the world. All those fliers posted through doors had clearly done their job. First my father opened a little office in town and Mum had to go down there and answer the telephone, then a shop appeared in the high street with the sign Preston's Electricals over the door.

My father took in electrical goods for repair and then he started selling them too. Eventually he opened a warehouse down by the docks to import washing machines, fridges and ovens. Money was obviously flowing freely, because by the time I was six, we moved from the flat into what seemed at the time to be a huge detached house in Treboeth, a grander part of Swansea.

Number 2 Brynawel Crescent was a tall, pebble-dashed building on the side of a hill looking down over the rooftops all the way to the sea. There was a steep terraced garden with a vegetable patch at the top and a brick wall that ran right round the edge, along which I used to tightrope walk tirelessly until I fell off one day and cut my nose.

Inside there were huge rooms which Mum decorated beautifully to my father's specifications.

There was a lot of purple carpet and lilac wallpaper and the lounge had a distinctly African feel. There was a bar in one corner with two elephant footstools, a drum with a glass top on it as a table, the maneless lion shot by my great, great-grandfather sneered from the wall and a pair of great big horns which might have been elephant tusks were arranged artistically as a focal point. The house also had a downstairs toilet – which we thought was unbelievable – three bedrooms and a cellar where Debbie and I loved to play. We called it the library. Almost best of all was the tiny and unique window in the shape of a cross fixed into the gable at the very top of the house. Even from a long way off, number 2 Brynawel Crescent stood out from all the other houses on the hillside because you could see the little glass cross glittering in the sun.

To go with the house my father treated himself to a gleaming new Jaguar car. And one day, in a fit of guilt about some particularly bad treatment of my mother, he bought Mum a little green Mini.

People looked at us from the outside and envied us. They took in the big house, the two cars, the mink coats and diamond rings my mother wore when she accompanied my father to glamorous functions in town and they thought we had everything. But they didn't realise that inside the big house we were tiptoeing round in fear whenever our father was home, that we seldom rode in the jaunty Jag and that, although my mother looked fabulous in front of my father's business cronies, she couldn't enjoy the glamorous nights out because she had to sit silently in the corner keeping her mouth shut. She was not allowed to speak.

Yes, people thought we had everything when really we had nothing. Nothing that counted anyway.

Why did my mother stay with him? It's a question her sister Kathleen always asked her. Even today Mum doesn't quite know the answer. 'I was a different person then,' she says. 'When I look back now, I don't know who I was.'

But the fact that my father was always shouting at her, 'You'll end up in the gutter with those children one of these days.' Or 'If you walk away from here, those kids will be taken off you and put in an orphanage,' probably had something to do with it.

Mum was the whole world to us and when we heard those terrible words Debbie and I would start to cry and cling frantically to her skirt, while Gary struggled manfully to suppress anxious tears.

'Don't go, Mum, don't leave us!' I'd sob hysterically.

'Stay, Mum! Stay!' Debbie wailed in terror alongside me, while Gary moved to block the front door, just in case.

And Mum was forced to hug us all and promise she'd never go. Which was just what my father wanted, of course.

More than anything Mum was desperate to protect us from him. She would accept any amount of abuse to distract him from lashing out at us. Yet at times he'd become so angry at some small misdemeanour of Gary's he'd rush up the stairs to lash out at him with his leather belt while Mum would be trying to drag his arm away. She was the one who invariably ended up with the worst bruises while the rest of us would be screaming and sobbing and begging him to stop.

Yet despite the emotional blackmail there came a time when Mum did decide to leave. I don't know what brought things to a head but one night, after my father had stormed out, Mum told us to put our coats and shoes on. Then she dragged the big old pushchair with squeaky springs out of the cupboard, loaded it with a few hastily packed bags and led us all out into the street.

'Where are we going, Mum?' asked Debbie in a scared voice, but Mum had started to cry and she didn't answer.

'Shut up, Debbie,' said Gary.

I squeezed her hand.

Mum started walking and we fell in quietly around her. The streets were very dark, it had started to rain and we set off down the hill, the wind sending sharp little pellets of water stinging into our faces.

After a while we came to Auntie Kathleen's. Mum left us at the gate with the pushchair and hurried to the door. Warm golden light from the hall spilled out over the step turning the two women into silhouettes, black cutouts against the doorway. I heard Auntie Kathleen's surprised voice of welcome suddenly change. Low, urgent conversation drifted down the path. Soft, sympathetic notes from my aunt; harsher, half-sobbing responses from Mum. Then, abruptly, mum turned and came hurrying back to us, snatching the pushchair from Debbie's grasp and setting it spinning down the road again.

'I'm sorry Pat . . . really . . .' Auntie Kathleen's words floated out to us as we walked briskly on. Mum didn't even look back. Tears were rolling down her face but she didn't seem to notice. She didn't even brush them away.

'Where are we going now, Mum?' Debbie whispered.

'Shut up, Debbie!' said Gary even louder, but there was a little shake in his voice and I knew he was scared as well. They were all scared. Even Mum. Yet oddly enough, although I was worried for Mum, I felt strangely calm about the whole adventure. Although I couldn't see him, I could sense the Lined Man nearby, hovering on the edge of our little group. 'It's all right,' he said softly in my ear, 'I'm taking care of you. Don't be afraid.' And I knew that whatever happened, we would come to no harm.

Next we came to the home of Mum's other sister, Auntie Marlene. But she too had the same reaction as Auntie Kathleen. No-one had room for a runaway wife with four children in tow; they had enough trouble finding space for their own kids. If only we weren't such a big family.

On and on we went. Mum called on all the people she could think of, but no-one could help. Perhaps they were afraid of my father coming round and breaking down the door; perhaps they feared we'd never leave.

On we trudged. Mum lifted me into the pushchair.

Debbie held the handle and the boys followed on behind. The rain drummed harder. Water rushed along the gutters and splashed into our shoes. Cars swooshed through the puddles showering us with muddy spray and the wind picked up, slapping our wet hair across our cheeks. The pushchair began to squeak agonisingly, as if in protest.

I started to shiver, so did Debbie. Gary crammed his fist into his mouth to still his chattering teeth. And on we went, Mum marching, head held high and rigid, a woman turned to stone. Up hills and down, along deserted high streets with shadow-laden shops and dissolving neon signs and out into the dark again.

Squeak, squeak, squeak went the pushchair, squelch, squelch, squelch went our feet. Then suddenly there was a thud, the rasp of metal on stone, my seat lurched heavily down and I saw a wheel rolling away down the road. Gary went racing after it, quickly brought it back and with cold, slippery fingers fixed it into place again. But it was all too much for my mother.

She gave a big sigh. Her shoulders heaved and then with an angry wrench she turned the treacherous pushchair round.

Not a word was spoken. Wet through and exhausted, we slogged wearily home. By the time my father staggered back from the pub we were all in bed, the pushchair towelled off and stowed back in the cupboard, our sodden coats and shoes drying out in the kitchen.

I wonder if he even knew.

How had it come to this? How could things have gone so wrong?

Mum met my father at a jive in Swansea. Mum was a pretty girl with a twenty-inch waist, jet black hair, big blue eyes and a cheeky sense of humour. My father was a dashing soldier in the Elvis Presley mould. In fact, Elvis was his hero and the young Alastair played up the resemblance for all he was worth.

With his tanned, muscular body, slicked back Elvis quiff, daring dark brown eyes and devastating smile he bowled Mum over. She was completely dazzled and fell in love more or less on the spot.

Physically, they looked a good match and when Alastair's sophisticated charm (or so it seemed to Mum) linked up with Mum's warm personality and infectious giggle, people thought they made the ideal couple.

The problem was that they came from wildly different backgrounds. My father, the son of a famous engineer in colonial Kenya, came from a wealthy family. He was accustomed to a luxury home, deferential neighbours and servants on hand to cater to his every whim. Educated at a posh boarding school, he expected to enjoy a brilliant future.

Mum's childhood, on the other hand, could not have been more different. Her devout Irish father, who at one time had intended to be a priest, brought his family to Swansea and then died when Mum was seven, leaving his wife to rear six children alone. Grandma took a job in a factory to make ends meet, but they were so poor the children had only one pair of knickers apiece to wash out and wear, there were bugs in the bed and meat was served only when guests came for dinner.

Mum was quite bright, but at the convent school where she was sent, the nuns sat the children in good clothes at the front of the class to read and write while the patched ragamuffins were put at the back with a pile of sewing. Mum got the sewing.

She had hoped to be a nurse one day but Grandma couldn't afford the training, so when Mum left school she was sent to work in a sewing factory. She didn't think much about the future, but if she did, her hopes weren't high.

Yet my mother and father did have one thing in common, though they seldom discussed it – both had suffered childhood traumas. When Mum was 11 she was crossing the busy Mumbles Road with her little brother Billy when, unnoticed by her, Billy bent down to tie his shoelaces. Mum reached the kerb and turned to speak to him just in time to see him still in the middle of the road with a lorry hurtling towards his crouching form. Even before she could scream, Billy was tossed into the air and disappeared under the screeching tyres. He died instantly. Mum's been terrified of roads every since.

And my father, for all his privilege, knew moments of horror too. He grew up in Kenya at the time when the Mau Mau terrorists, bent on independence, were staging bloody atrocities on both the white settlers and their African sympathisers. Tales circulated of how the Mau Mau loved to come across a pregnant woman –

they'd rip the baby from her womb and eat it, it was claimed. True or not, everyone dreaded coming out of their house in the morning to find a dead cat hanging from the gate post. It was a sinister sign which meant the killers would soon be back to do the same to you.

Perhaps such experiences created an unspoken bond between them, who can tell? But they were in love, though the match was not received well by either family. The Prestons felt Mum was beneath them and must be marrying my father for his money – or the money they thought she believed he would one day inherit, because he certainly didn't seem to have any other source of income than his meagre soldier's pay back then – while Mum's mother took an instant dislike to the smiling young soldier from the moment he was first presented to her.

'He'll end up leaving you with four children,' said Grandma scornfully after my father had gone. Which was very perceptive of her, because that's exactly what he did.

But at the time neither my mother nor my father cared. They married in Swansea with only two friends present as witnesses and settled down to wedlock.

I don't how long it was before my father started to see Mum in the same light as his parents did, but gradually he must have come to regard her as embarrassingly uneducated, and by the time I came along, he was already treating her as a particularly incompetent servant. He wandered round the house dropping clothes, keys and personal items wherever he happened to be and Mum was expected to run around after him picking them up.

He inspected the house for traces of dust or dirty marks and although Mum cleaned frantically from dawn till dusk, he always found some minuscule blemish to rant about. And woe betide her if he lost something. The number of times we'd hear an outraged bellow from the bedroom, 'Someone's stolen my shoes!' and we'd all have to scurry around looking for them before he started lashing out at the imagined culprit.

By the age of eight, I had taken to going off for long walks by myself (it was much safer in those days for children to wander unaccompanied) and my favourite destination was a little house about fifteen minutes away which I christened 'the happy house'. White painted and pretty, it stood back from the road surrounded by neat little lawns, a rose arch and radiant flower beds. There were green shutters at the windows and a little green bench outside the door, and as evening fell they put the lights on without drawing the curtains and you could see inside. A couple of children and a mum and dad often gathered round the table, heads bent over a meal or a jigsaw puzzle and sometimes you could hear the sound of muffled laughter coming through the glass.

Best of all was what you couldn't see or hear. Great waves of happiness seemed to roll out from the very walls of that house and wash over me as I stood there half hidden by the hedge.

I never spoke to them, I don't know who they were

and they probably never knew I was there, but the happy family in the happy house fascinated me and I went to look at them often.

'So that's what it must be like,' I thought to myself, and I longed to live there too.

Bedtime had ceased to be a matter to dread. As time passed I'd become accustomed to the Lined Man's visits. He never hurt me or did me any harm and since he was always telling me that he was looking after me, he obviously cared. In fact, it got to the point where if for some reason he didn't come, or arrived later than usual, I began to find the silence rather dull. Boring even.

'Where are you? Are you there?' I'd whisper into the darkness and instantly his voice would come back: 'Yes, I'm here. Whenever you want me I'll be here.'

My fear melted away and was replaced by curiosity. My strange friend was clearly not like ordinary friends, so perhaps could he do things that ordinary people could not? I wondered what amazing powers he might have and I set about testing him.

'If you're so clever,' I said one night, 'tell me what I'm going to wear tomorrow.'

'Tomorrow you'll be wearing your dark blue dress,' the man replied.

Huh! I thought to myself, caught you out there. I knew he was wrong because that particular dress, a smart affair in deep blue with a matching blue-and-white striped tie had been a great favourite of mine and I'd literally worn it to death. It was now falling apart at the seams and Mum refused to let me wear it any more.

Of all the things I could put on tomorrow, it most certainly wouldn't be that dress.

Next morning I bounced out of bed, pulled on a jumper and jeans and with a smug smile went to find Mum. She was in the kitchen writing out a shopping list.

'Right,' she said, folding up the square of paper and putting it in her purse, 'No complaints, we're going to Morriston shopping and if you're good you can have a bag of cockles.'

We always groaned about a trip to Morriston because it was a long walk, Mum trailed us in and out of every single shop and then we had to carry the heavy bags back home. So she'd got into the habit of bribing us with a bag of cockles from one of the cockle ladies who paraded the streets in their long dresses and head-scarves with big cloth-covered baskets over their arms. A bag of their delicious salty little shellfish would keep us quiet most of the way home.

'Oh, and Diane, go and change. You can wear your blue dress.'

My knees almost collapsed under me.

'My blue dress? But you said I couldn't wear it any more. It's worn out!'

'I know,' said Mum with a big pleased smile, 'but look what I've done.'

And she went and got the dress from her room. She held it up to show me. It was all pressed and lovely, miraculously restored to its former blue and white glory.

'I've been up half the night mending that,' she said. 'I knew you'd be happy.'

Happy? I was speechless.

On another occasion I told the Lined Man I wanted to see where he came from. He didn't answer for a moment and I thought nothing was going to happen, then suddenly there was a whooshing sensation and I was flying again – just like when we went to Africa. The night rippled along my arms and legs, there was a breeze in my face and an impression of stars and then I was looking down on this glowing, bright scene. I could see a lake and crowds of people wandering about the far shore.

Then my feet touched gold-green grass that felt like the softest sponge and I was walking first towards the lake, and then somehow straight out across it right on top of the shining water. It didn't seem odd that my toes weren't even wet.

A gentle air of peace and contentment seemed to rest over the whole place and I stepped out of the lake onto the grass and into the smiling people. It seemed the most natural thing in the world to be there and no-one looked surprised to see me.

'Have you been here long?' I remember asking one woman who was standing with a child.

'It's as if it was a lifetime,' she said cheerfully.

Then I realised there were no animals anywhere.

'Where are the animals?' I asked, and even as I said the words I caught sight of a movement out of the corner of my eye and I turned to see hundreds and hundreds of dogs rushing towards me – Dalmatians, poodles, mongrels – dogs of every type pelting helter-skelter over the grass. Then at the last minute, just as I thought they were going to run me down, they disappeared into thin air.

It was as if you could summon up whatever you wanted in this place, I thought, and then I seemed to drift off to sleep.

The next morning I woke up in my own bed and I couldn't decide if it was a beautiful dream or if I'd really been there. It had seemed so real, yet not so much as a blade of golden grass crushed between my toes remained to prove the case either way. But then, perhaps it didn't matter. Whether it was in a dream or a genuine visit, I'd seen the place where the Lined Man came from and it looked good to me.

Chapter Five

It was Saturday morning, Dad was out at the warehouse and everyone was relaxed. Mum and Debbie were in the kitchen making jam tarts, Gary was messing about on his bike and I was in the lounge, back turned on the unfriendly lion head, pretending to be a pop star.

The radio was turned up loud and I was singing away into my hairbrush when I suddenly had the tingly feeling in the back of my neck that I was being watched. I looked round and there was a little girl standing behind me. She was a bit smaller than me with big blue eyes and the most beautiful dark brown hair – glossy and gleaming as patent leather. She was wearing something white and she was so lovely she almost glowed. I'd never seen her before, yet she seemed oddly familiar. She looked a little bit like my sister Debbie and a little bit like me. Despite this there was something about the radiance that clung to her that reminded me of the people in the beautiful land where the Lined Man came from. I knew now, because he'd taken me there, that his home was some heaven-like place, so this girl must be a spirit girl I decided. Which was fine by me.

The girl smiled this exquisite smile, and though her lips didn't seem to move I somehow heard her say: 'I'm your sister.' And then she was gone.

I didn't doubt her for a moment. The family resemblance was so strong. I was thrilled. So I wasn't the youngest after all – I had another sister! I rushed off to tell Mum.

'Mum!' I cried excitedly, bursting into the kitchen where she was dusting flour onto Debbie's pastry board for her, 'I've got a little sister!'

Normally Mum hardly listened to my nonsense – attention-seeking she called it – but today her reaction was strange. Her face seemed to go pale and she turned away sharply. 'Don't be so silly, Diane.'

'But Mum, I saw her! She's got dark hair like yours and blue ey . . .'

'Diane, be quiet! That's enough of your stories. Now go and play!'

Debbie rolled her eyes and Mum sounded quite cross. She began bashing the pastry so ferociously I reluctantly went back to my singing.

But that wasn't the end of it. Not long afterwards, another sister came to see me, accompanied by two dark-haired little boys who also claimed to be part of the family. My new brothers looked very similar to Gary. The four of them took to dropping in regularly to say hello and they always told me one of them was celebrating a birthday.

For some reason Mum found this news particularly

upsetting when I eagerly passed it on. In fact she got angry.

'Diane, shut up!' she'd eventually yell, and sometimes she'd rush out of the room. I couldn't understand it.

It was only years later that I discovered the truth. Dad had made up his mind to have no further children after I'd somehow slipped through the net, so he'd used his brutality to end four further pregnancies. Mum was a Catholic and Dad didn't like using contraceptives, so if nature had been allowed to take its course they would have had not four children, but eight. What they didn't realise then, of course, was that they still did.

It wasn't long after this that life looked up a little. Uncle Leon, or rather Great-uncle Leon, came to stay. Things had evidently turned nasty in Africa and Uncle Leon, my grandfather's brother who used to run a chicken farm, had lost everything and had come to Wales to start again. My father's business was doing well by this time and the Kenyan branch of the family no doubt expected him to help out. My father, who never could pass up an opportunity to impress people with grand gestures or to show off his wealth, agreed that Leon could come and live with us. He probably reckoned that his old uncle might come in useful as an odd-job-man-cum-baby-sitter.

A small caravan was installed in the garden as a home (there were limits to hospitality after all), and a long wire was put in, running from the caravan through our kitchen window to the electric socket indoors so that Uncle Leon could power his lights and small fire.

We children were delighted with him. We'd never seen anyone quite like Uncle Leon before. He was a funny little man with deeply tanned skin, false teeth that dropped out when he ate, thick-rimmed glasses and a big hairy mole on his arm. When we asked what the mole was he'd always say he'd been bitten by a snake. But he was immensely kind and he worshipped Mum. Every time she ventured into the garden with a basket of washing, Uncle Leon came diving out of his caravan to let down the line for her. He would stand there patiently while she pegged out the wet clothes and then reverently put the line up again.

Every night Mum cooked an extra dinner for Uncle Leon and she flashed the kitchen lights to let him know it was ready. At first he came over to eat round the table with us but we giggled so much when his false teeth fell out that we'd be sent to bed. In the end we missed so many suppers because we just couldn't help ourselves that for the sake of our health, Uncle Leon decided to eat in the caravan.

He was very fond of us even though we plagued him terribly. Sometimes when he wasn't looking we hid his glasses under a cushion and pretended we had no idea where they'd gone.

'I know it's you ruddy lot,' he'd say – ruddy being Uncle Leon's crossest word – 'Where've you ruddy lot hidden my glasses? Ruddy little cows you!'

And we just giggled all the more.

At other times, if Mum and Dad weren't about, we waited till it got dark and Uncle Leon was reading in his caravan, then we'd switch his electric wire off, plunging him into blackness. And just to make things more interesting, we turned off all the lights in the house as well, so that he had to blunder about in the shadows to find the socket.

In he'd come, muttering under his breath. He'd fumble about for a bit, then the lights would spring on and off he'd go back to his caravan. We'd wait till he'd sat down then we'd do it again. And again. And again. Five or six times we'd turn his lights off, then we'd scatter and run to hide and Uncle Leon would be 'ruddying' all over the house looking for us.

'You ruddy lot!' we could hear him complain as he puffed up and down the stairs, 'I'm going to have you ruddy lot!'

And we almost burst with the effort of stifling our laughter. Uncle Leon was the gentlest of men and we weren't frightened at all.

I think Uncle Leon was quite distressed when he heard the way my father spoke to Mum and saw her bruises, but, living under my father's roof, he never dared confront him. The only time he ever plucked up courage to voice his disapproval, my father angrily threatened to pack him off back to Africa. After that Uncle Leon bit his lip. 'Ruddy bast . . .' you'd hear from the corner of his mouth, 'ruddy bast . . .' but then he'd turn away in disgust.

Uncle Leon's friend Kay, though, was quite a different matter. Kay arrived from Africa to spend a week or two with Leon and ended up staying a year.

Kay was tall and slim, towering above Uncle Leon like a craggy tree. She talked like a man in a voice that was husky but posh and she smoked like a trooper. She had big yellow teeth that protruded and the largest feet we'd ever seen on a woman. My father's slippers often lay around the house and Kay would dare to put them on.

She used to bring her washing into the kitchen for Mum to do and somewhere in the pile there were always several pairs of great big bloomers, quite unlike the dainty little lace-trimmed scraps my mother wore. Horrible children that we were, how we guffawed at those outsize bloomers. Could it be that she was really a man, we wondered? When we thought she wasn't looking, we used to squint at her chest to see if we could discern any boobs through her sensible shirt. But we could never be certain.

But Kay was as kind as Uncle Leon and she wasn't afraid of my father. 'Alastair, could you leave Pat alone please,' she'd command in her deep, posh voice when Dad started picking on Mum and for a while at least, my father fell silent.

The relationship between Kay and Uncle Leon intrigued us. We used to tiptoe out to the caravan to peep through the window to see if they were sleeping together. Kay said they weren't, and we never caught them in the same bed, but I couldn't understand how they could live in such a tiny caravan without sharing the bed. There was only one.

We particularly enjoyed the evenings when Mum and Dad went out and Uncle Leon and Kay babysat.

They didn't mind what mischief we got up to, or where we went, and they even joined in our games of hide and seek. When Uncle Leon had to find me, my brothers put me in the big airing cupboard at the top of the stairs because there was a tiny space on top of the tank that only I could fit into. Then they locked the door and it seemed like hours before anyone came to get me out.

When I was the finder it was a different story. As I counted to twenty while they all ran off I'd close my eyes and suddenly a picture of Debbie squeezed under the bed came into my mind. I'd go straight to her. Then I'd think about Gary and an image of Gary standing behind the curtain appeared. Laughing, I'd run to the curtain, pull it back and there he was. I was so good at discovering their hiding places that they didn't want to play with me. They thought I was cheating, but of course I wasn't – I didn't know how I did it, the pictures just leapt into my head.

Soon after he arrived Uncle Leon decided to get a parrot. We already had a pet, a beautiful cream and gold Lassie dog called Simba – because he had a big cream mane like a lion's. Simba had caused a bit of a problem when he first arrived. My father walked in with this tiny puppy one day – goodness knows why, it was unheard of for him to bring us a nice surprise – and without thinking, my mother put down a saucer of milk for the little scrap. But the milk was ice cold, straight from the fridge, and after gulping it greedily Simba began to shiver and shake.

'You stupid woman!' shouted my father, belting Mum

across the face, 'Don't you know better than to give a puppy cold milk! It should be warm. That's a valuable dog and you'll kill it the way you go on!' And he hit her again.

We were horrified. Gary stepped forward to try to protect Mum but my father pushed him contemptuously aside and Mum, as ever more worried about Gary and the dog than her own bruises, shushed Gary away and rushed to fetch a warm towel to wrap round Simba. She tucked him up in front of the fire and then heated some fresh milk on the stove. It wasn't long before the puppy was completely recovered and trotting round the room chasing our delighted feet.

But Uncle Leon clearly felt that while dogs were okay, no home was complete without a parrot. One day a little brown box arrived with the morning post – the odd thing about this box was that it was squawking.

The four of us crowded round Uncle Leon on tiptoe as he carefully snipped off the brown paper and lifted the lid. Packed inside, slightly crumpled, was a little grey parrot all the way from Africa. Uncle Leon fetched a big golden cage from his caravan and gently stood the parrot inside. The bird shook itself huffily, clambered up onto the wooden perch and began fluffing out its squashed plumage, squawking loudly all the while.

'What's its name, Uncle Leon?' asked Debbie, waggling her finger through the bars to attract the bird's attention. The parrot ignored her.

'She hasn't got a name yet,' said Uncle Leon. 'What would you like to call her?'

'Polly,' said Debbie.

So Polly it was.

Strictly speaking Polly was Uncle Leon's pet, but since his caravan was so small her cage was kept in our dining room. Uncle Leon came over every day to clean her out, feed her apples, seeds and even chillies – which she seemed to enjoy – and to let her have a good flap around the room.

For a while Polly did nothing but squawk, but then one morning we heard the words, 'Simba, sit!' coming from the dining room in a voice similar to my mother's, yet not my mother's. Intrigued, we trooped into the dining room to find Simba sitting obediently in front of the parrot's cage.

Polly bossed Simba around quite a bit after that. She also took to commanding, 'Debbie! Diane! Stop it! I said, stop it!'

And once she yelled, 'Alastair! Alastair!' so convincingly that my father, who was in the bath, came rushing out dressed in a dripping towel in the belief that he must be wanted on the phone. When he discovered it was only the parrot, he was livid.

'Stupid woman!' he snarled, grabbing Mum by the hair as she tried to slide away, 'Don't teach the parrot to say stupid things like that.'

Increased prosperity did nothing to improve Dad's temper and when Uncle Leon finally moved away to a flat of his own, taking Polly with him, my father returned to his old spiteful ways.

My brothers increasingly annoyed him. If he detected

the faintest hint of defiance in their voices he'd drag off the leather belt he'd bought in Spain and rush up the stairs to thrash them with it. Mum would try to get in between them but would be thrown aside, landing in a sobbing heap on the hall carpet. Gary made a point of refusing to cry out when he was beaten. He didn't want to give Dad the satisfaction of knowing he was hurt, but Debbie and I would listen to the thrashes through the wall, trembling in terror and pulling the covers over our heads.

Lesser offences were punished with lines. Gary regularly received lines: 'I must not cheek my mother.' 'I must go to bed immediately I'm asked.' 'I must tidy my room.' And so on.

Yet brutal as he was, my father never raised his hand to me. He abused everyone under his roof except me, and I wasn't afraid of him. Looking back I can't understand why this should have been. Was it the protection of the Lined Man? Could my father somehow sense some other presence around me? Or could he see I had no fear for myself and it made him ashamed? Who can tell? All I knew was that I felt as if I was sealed in a safe little bubble and he couldn't hurt me. In fact at times it almost seemed as if he was more scared of me than I was of him, small as I was.

He never hit me and he only ever gave me lines once. One evening Mum said it was bedtime and I made a fuss as usual, but this time my father heard me. Furiously he sent me upstairs with the others to complete a hundred lines of: 'I must go to bed when

I'm told.' But I was still not a confident writer and this was a difficult task for me. So I fetched a ruler and pencil and quickly drew out one hundred nice straight lines on a sheet of paper.

'You can't give him that,' said Gary aghast, when he saw what I'd done. 'He'll go mad.'

But I knew I couldn't do anything else. So I went back down and nervously handed the lines to my father. He stared at the paper for a long time. Then he looked at me and I looked straight back at him. There was a deep silence. Was he going to explode? He looked at the lines once more. 'Okay,' he said at last, putting the paper down on the table. 'And next time, you go to bed when your mother tells you.'

He never gave me lines again.

As I walked out of the room Gary and Debbie were lined up in the hall listening. 'Typical!' said Gary when I emerged. 'She's got away with it again!'

'It's because she's the baby,' said Debbie.

And maybe that was it. I was so small for my age even my father would have felt a bully to hit me.

Another evening Mum was out at a Tupperware party and, unusually, my father was at home, supposedly looking after us. I was in bed, Debbie was in the bath and my father was downstairs watching television and drinking beer from his bar.

'Debbie!' he suddenly roared in that off-key, blurry tone his voice took on after a few drinks, 'Get down here and mend the TV!'

Debbie didn't answer.

'Debbie!' he shouted again. 'COME DOWN HERE!'

There was a splash as Debbie jumped out of the bath, but she didn't go downstairs. She ran into our bedroom, leapt onto the bunk and sat there huddled in her towel, soaking wet and trembling so violently the bed shook.

'DEBBIE!' he bellowed, angrier than ever. 'If you don't get down here NOW, I'm going to come up there and fetch you and then you'll be sorry.'

Debbie's teeth were chattering and the bed shook harder than ever. She shrank back against the wall, dripping hair spreading damp across the blue paper.

The Lined Man was suddenly next to me. 'The TV's not broken,' he murmured in my ear, 'he's pulled the aerial out himself.'

That twisted feeling in my stomach tightened another notch. Waves of some dark, deeply unpleasant emotion were flowing up the stairs and I could tell that something horrible was going to happen if I didn't act fast. Terror vibrated through the air, the whole room seemed to quiver and I could feel my own hands start to shake. I wasn't afraid of my father, but I was petrified of what he might do to Debbie.

'Don't go down Debbie!' I said. 'Stay here.'

But the next second we heard the lounge door burst open and my father's furious feet were thumping from step to step. Debbie began to moan in fear. I leapt out of my bunk and raced to the bedroom door just as my father crashed through it. I barely reached his chest but I stood in front of him barring his path.

'Debbie!' he yelled over my head, beer fumes shooting in all directions. 'Get downstairs now!'

'She's not coming!' I squeaked up at him, locking my knees to stop them knocking. 'And if you don't leave her alone, I'm going to go down that road and tell everybody I see that you're going to hurt Debbie.'

'Get out of my way,' he growled.

But I didn't move. 'I mean it,' I said, 'I'm going to tell everyone. I'll shout as loud as I can! I'll scream! Everyone will know you're going to hurt Debbie.'

For a second he glared at me wildly, as if he'd knock me out of the way. He raised his hand and then suddenly he stopped. The crazy glint faded from his eyes and he faltered. He stood there uncertainly for a second or two, a confused look growing on his face. Then his hand dropped and he turned.

'Stupid kids,' he muttered. 'You wait. You just wait, that's all.'

And he lumbered away back downstairs.

I climbed into Debbie's bunk and we hugged each other tightly until we both fell asleep.

I didn't know what was wrong but my father seemed to be getting worse. There was one melodrama after another. One night I heard hysterical screaming from the kitchen and went down to find my father holding an air-gun to Mum's head while my brother and sister were hopping about around him, almost beside themselves, begging him not to shoot.

It was an alarming sight and yet I felt curiously

unmoved. I just knew it was a bluff. 'Take no notice,' said the Lined Man in my ear, so I knew I was right.

I looked coolly at my father. Ever since the Debbie episode I could hardly bring myself so much as to glance at him, but now I stared into his tanned, perspiring face.

'He's not going to shoot,' I said calmly.

'Aren't I?' A wolfish grin danced around his mouth.

'No,' I said.

He jabbed the gun into Mum's temple one more time. Then let it fall away.

'Hah!' he laughed. 'It's not even loaded. Let that be a lesson to you. Next time it might be.' And chuckling to himself at his excellent joke, he walked away swinging the gun like an old-time cowboy.

At other times the situation was more serious. When he was genuinely drunk he became completely irrational and as always Mum's greatest fear was that he would turn on us children.

One particularly dreadful night after another vicious row, he hit on the perfect way of getting at Mum. He threatened to kill us kids. Whether he was serious or not I couldn't tell that time, but Mum believed him. Ushering us into a cowering group behind her she grabbed a sharp knife from the kitchen drawer and stood there in front of him slashing her own arms with it.

'Look, Alastair! Look!' she cried, trying to divert his eyes from us to the bright red blood spurting from her skin.

Distracted, he stopped to watch the flashing blade and we slipped quietly away.

Why Mum never turned the knife on him I can't imagine, but her spirit wasn't completely broken. In fact, in her own quiet way she even got her own back on him. There had been yet another drunken night and I happened to wake up when he came staggering home from the pub. Peeping though the crack in our bedroom door I saw him zig-zagging up the stairs, brown tie askew, belly hanging over his trousers. At the top, he took off his shiny leather shoes and threw them one after the other over his shoulder. Down they flew, bouncing, thump-thump off the wall and making Simba bark.

'Shut up, Simba!' shouted my father as he stumbled across the landing and fell into bed.

Mum must have been biding her time in the bedroom pretending to be asleep. She often waited for moments like these to collect the housekeeping. Despite dressing her in furs and diamonds for business functions, my father was very mean with his money the rest of the time. Mum wasn't allowed to have any cash for herself and was given just enough to buy food, but if she needed extra funds for birthday gifts or new shoes for us children she had to resort to hazardous tactics.

Once my father was snoring, she crept out of bed and crawled across the monkey skin rug to the chair where my father threw his trousers. Then she'd gently ease them to the carpet, tease out from the pocket the fat roll of notes he liked to wave about, carefully peel off a couple and then softly replace the trousers on the chair.

This particular night she was unlucky. He stirred and caught her. There was an outraged yell and the sound of blows.

'Thief! You dirty little thief!' he screamed. 'Get out of my house! Go on! Get out! No, don't you dare try to get back into bed. Get out! Get back to the gutter where you belong.'

I could hear crying, more terrifying blows and then silence. A few minutes later heavy snores resumed.

Worried that Mum must be hurt I slipped along the hall to their room. And there she was crouched in the corner, sobbing silently, her face all blotchy and red, a tissue held to her lips to muffle the sound.

'Mum!' I whispered.

She jumped, alarm leaping into her eyes.

'Shhhh,' she said softly, wiping away tears, 'go back to bed now. I'm all right. Really I'm all right. Go on back to bed. Don't wake your father.' She was desperately afraid that if I did, he might turn on me.

Reluctantly, I tiptoed away but Mum stayed there all night crouched in the corner, not daring to return to the bed.

Next morning, however, in that miraculous way she had, Mum was up and in the kitchen as usual as if nothing had happened.

'Today,' she said with a smile, 'we're going to do some baking. Debbie, run up to the blue van and get a tin of cat food would you.'

The blue van was a mobile shop run by a neighbour of ours who lived up the hill. He preferred to sell his wares from the back of the van as he drove around his beat, but he could usually be persuaded to unlock the shop after hours for some desperate and forgetful neighbour.

'Cat food?' repeated Debbie. 'But we don't have a cat Mum.'

'Never mind,' said Mum taking the bag of flour from the cupboard and setting out her pastry board. 'Run along.'

Maybe she was going to try a new diet for Simba, we thought.

Debbie ran and I stayed to help Mum with the baking. I stood around passing her the lard, fetching the big pie dish, unwrapping the steak and generally making myself useful. If I was good I might earn a few off-cuts for Debbie and me to make our own jam tarts.

By the time Debbie returned, Mum had lined the dish with pastry and filled it with steak, onions and gravy.

'Lovely,' she said, taking the cat food from Debbie. Then she opened the tin, scraped out every pungent fishy scrap and ladled it into the pie. She gave it a big stir, mixing the cat food thoroughly into the beef and placed the floury lid over the top.

'Mum!' gasped Debbie, half horrified, half delighted.

'Mum!' I cried in mock alarm, then I started to giggle, Debbie joined in and soon the three of us were rocking around the kitchen laughing our heads off.

Mum cut beautiful pastry leaves and arranged them round the centre of the pie, then she crimped the edges with the utmost care and painted the whole lot gleaming gold with beaten egg. By the time she'd finished it was the most magnificent pie you ever saw and we were crying with laughter.

We could hardly contain ourselves until lunchtime when the pie was served. Mum cut a nice big slice and took it into father on a tray as usual and we squashed outside the door, treading on each other's feet, peering through the crack to watch him eat it. When he took a big forkful and put it into his mouth, we exploded with mirth.

'You lot! Bed!' came the expected order and we pattered off still laughing.

Mum didn't dare let us disturb our father on Saturday afternoons when he had his nap on the sofa, because if anyone woke him up he'd punch out automatically in a bizarre sort of reflex action. Should she ever need to call him urgently to the phone she had to stand a safe distance away at the door and lob the green velvet scatter cushions at him. So now we had to wait until he woke up to find out what had happened. As usual it was me who was sent in.

My father was sitting there, TV tuned to the football results, checking his coupons. He looked perfectly healthy.

'Did you enjoy your dinner?' I asked nonchalantly, aware of the others guffawing silently behind the door.

'Yes,' he said. 'Why? WHY?'

'No reason. It just looked nice. Smelled nice. There's plenty more. Would you like another piece?'

My father scowled at me suspiciously.

'Pat!' he shouted, 'what have you done to that pie?'

He never did get to the bottom of the pie mystery. In fact he ate another slice for his tea, but sadly it didn't give him so much as indigestion. We could only conclude that the pet food companies had been telling the truth all along – pet food really is okay for humans too.

We happily relived Mum's revenge many times in the following months. Hugging it to ourselves in secret joy. We felt like conspirators, like the underground resistance, but in truth the situation wasn't a laughing matter. Mum became more and more unhappy.

While my father was out Auntie Kathleen, accompanied by Peter, came for frequent amateur counselling sessions. Peter, now a tall lad of 14, was despatched to amuse Debbie and me in the lounge while Mum and Auntie Kathleen huddled together over a pot of tea in the kitchen. Mum would often end up in tears and once, coming in and finding her dabbing at her eyes with a tissue, kind-hearted Peter put his arms round her.

'Don't worry Auntie Pat,' he said, 'life won't always be like this for you.'

And he was right. But things got worse before they got better. There was even a night when, goaded beyond endurance and with no means of escaping, Mum climbed out of the boys' bedroom window onto the roof of our kitchen extension with the intention of throwing herself off and committing suicide. I'm not sure that it was actually high enough for the fall to kill her, but she could have certainly done herself a lot of damage and, once again, the four of us were gathered round the windowpane in distress, begging her to come in. Which, after an hour or so, she did.

Yet oddly enough, for all my father's brutality towards her, it was infidelity that finally made Mum decide enough was enough.

One evening we were sitting together in the lounge; Dad was out as usual, Mum was watching a soap, Debbie was doing her homework and I was colouring. Then an odd thing happened. I was vigorously applying orange felt pen to the curly mane of a prancing pony when suddenly the pony wobbled out of my vision and I was looking at a pub. A crowd of people were standing around drinking and over in the corner a couple were snuggled on a banquette, heads close. The woman had silvery blonde hair, vivid turquoise eye-shadow and a short skirt and she was twizzling a little red cherry on a stick round and round in her glass. She was giggling up into the face of her dark-haired companion and he was smiling suavely back at her. And when he turned his head slightly I saw that it was my father.

I jumped at the sight of him and dropped my orange felt pen. Instantly the pub disappeared and my pony came back.

'Mum!' I cried, 'Dad's in the pub with a lady with blonde hair!'

'Diane! Honestly,' said Mum, 'your stories. Don't talk about your father like that.'

'But he is,' I protested. 'I saw him.'

'Now that's quite enough. How could you possibly have seen him? Just shut up.'

'But . . .'

'Enough!' snapped Mum, but there was alarm in her eyes.

Not long after that, the phone calls started. Day after day when Dad was at work an unknown woman phoned Mum. 'You're no good to him,' she used to say, 'He doesn't care about you. He'd be much better off with me.'

No doubt she'd seen Mum's diamonds and minks, the smart Jag and the big house, and decided she was in with a chance of winning them for herself. If only she knew what she was letting herself in for.

There were further rows, violence and denials in equal measure from my father, but the woman kept phoning and in the end he was forced to admit the truth.

Shell-shocked, Mum summoned the strength to go and see a solicitor and with bewildering speed our lives changed forever.

For several days Dad didn't come home at all, then one afternoon he turned up with his colleagues from work and a van. Mum, the boys and Debbie ran and barricaded themselves in the bedroom Debbie and I shared and refused to come out. Dad shouted and roared for a bit but nothing happened and presumably he didn't want to look bad in front of his workmates, so he gave up and turned his attention instead to directing operations as his men cleared the house and loaded our furniture into the van. No-one took the slightest notice of me. My father stared straight through me as if I was invisible, which was fine by me. I was left in peace simply to watch as the men worked.

Out went the stuffed animal heads, the drum table, the bar stools and just about everything else. Dad went upstairs, ransacked Mum's dressing table and found the jewels she'd tried to hide inside her clothes. Then he rolled up the monkey skin rug and carried that down to the van.

Our home was disappearing in front of my eyes, but I didn't care. I hated those dusty old dead animals anyway. Yet I thought Mum would be upset and so I was determined to save her something. While he was at the van I ran from room to room trying to hide a few small items. I pushed ornaments behind the curtains where he wouldn't see them and I grabbed the pretty porcelain lady in a crinoline skirt that I remembered my father once saying was quite valuable, sat down on the sofa, which for some reason he didn't bother to take, and hid her behind my cushion.

When they eventually slammed the front door for the last time the house was bare but the porcelain lady was still intact, one stiff arm sticking into my back through the dralon.

Mum and the rest of the family finally emerged and crept down the stairs to survey the devastation. Mum's lips quivered as she took in the empty rooms and the marks on the wallpaper where the pictures and animal heads had been, but she smiled bravely.

'Well, that'll save on the dusting,' she said.

'And we've still got this, Mum!' I added, pulling out the porcelain lady with a flourish like a magician.

She laughed and gave me a hug. The important thing, as we all knew, was that we'd got each other. My father had gone. All that was left of him was a row of wire coat hangers in the wardrobe swinging from the rail where his shirts had been.

Chapter Six

I was eleven when my childhood began. I hadn't realised it before but up until that point I was a sort of pre-adult, my undersized shoulders drooping with the weight of trying to protect my family, despite the fact that I was the youngest of them all.

They didn't know what I was doing, of course, and I couldn't see it myself at the time. All I understood then was that whenever my father was in the house, Debbie and in particular my Mum needed a help that only I could give. I'd realised that when I appeared, my father seemed to slink away instead of lashing out, so I felt I always had to be close by to get between them if he came in. I was like a little guard dog, circling them constantly, one ear always cocked, even when I was asleep, for sounds of danger. And then in the blink of an eye, it was gone. Light flooded the house and suddenly the rooms were full of laughter. We sang. We talked at the table. We giggled. We coughed. We even made jokes.

The knot deep inside me gradually melted away and my stomach felt weightless as if it might float. I slept the whole night through without listening for the dread sound of my father's key in the lock and I started to grow. My sleeves rode higher and higher up my arms, my socks fell further down my legs and my toes pressed hard against the end of my shoes. But I didn't care. I skipped up the street and tightrope-walked around the garden wall, happy in the knowledge that no angry bellow was going to interrupt my games.

Debbie and I ran wild. We spent our weekends making houses out of cardboard boxes along the banks of the nearby stream or we climbed to the little church on top of the hill and rearranged the graveyard. Some of the graves were crammed with flowers while others were neglected and overgrown, their mossy headstones peering forlornly out between a tangle of straggly stinging nettles. This didn't seem fair to Debbie and me, so we spent many a happy hour sharing out the flowers from the abundant 'haves' around the graves of the poor forgotten 'have-nots'. By the time we'd finished the whole churchyard had a bright and cheerful look.

I even adopted one particular grave. This was an especially sad 'have-not' who didn't appear to have been visited for a very long time. One day, as I was arranging daffodils at the foot of the headstone, an old woman's voice said, 'They're nice dear. That looks much better.'

I glanced round but the only other person in sight was Debbie, a few graves away, carefully threading tulips into a stone vase with pepper-pot holes on the top.

I tried to read the name on the faded stone above my

daffodils but it was almost worn away. Nevertheless, I was sure it belonged to a lady.

'I'm glad you like them,' I told her, 'I'll get you some more next week. There's always loads by Sunday evening.'

'I'd like that,' said my new friend.

I was quite accustomed by now to talking to people who I couldn't see and if this lady was some sort of ghost it didn't worry me. She wasn't at all scary. Children are very accepting of things that adults might regard as strange, but it seemed quite simple to me. Although we didn't go to church, Mum was a Catholic and she'd told us about baby Jesus and Heaven where good people went after they died. It seemed natural to me that the owners of these graves were in heaven, and if they popped back from time to time to chat to the odd visitor who could hear them, it was perfectly understandable. I'd probably do the same myself. The only frustrating thing for them, I imagined, was that so few people seemed to be able to hear them. Perhaps you needed special ears, like those of a dog that could pick up the sound of a dog whistle, inaudible to everyone else. Maybe I'd been born with dog ears, I thought! And cat eyes, too, for that matter, since I could also see things other people couldn't see.

Every week after that I made a point of decorating the old lady's grave with extra special care. I decided that she must be my grandma. Debbie and I were always sad that we'd never had a granny. Our mother's mother had died before I was born, when my father was still stationed with the army in Germany, and Mum was forever desolate that he hadn't allowed her to come home for the funeral, so she never discovered exactly where the grave was.

As for our father's mother, she'd divorced my grandfather and gone to live in Scotland years before our visit to Kenya. We only saw her once. I was about eight when my father announced that she was coming to stay. Debbie and I got so excited that we were going to have a granny at last. We were looking forward to a little white-haired old lady with knitting, just like the picture in our Red Riding Hood book, but instead this huge, 6ft-tall Amazon with big feet and a gun-metal bob arrived. She took no notice of us and lay in bed all day. After she left, Mum found a load of vodka bottles under her bed so we knew she couldn't have been a real granny at all.

Our graveyard Granny, we convinced ourselves, was the genuine article. I decided that we'd found the place where Mum's mother was buried and we took to visiting her often. Sometimes we even brought a picnic so we could have tea with her. Debbie and I used to make ourselves comfortable on either side of the little cracked stone kerb, drape some newly-scrounged blooms across the grave and then settle down to eat egg sandwiches and tell Granny about our day.

Debbie could never hear Granny's side of the conversation, but it didn't matter because I used to relay what she said. I don't think Debbie really believed I was talking to a real person in Heaven but she was quite happy to go along with the game. 'Let's pretend' was always one of our favourite ways of passing the time.

For the first time in our lives we were truly happy. Money was scarce but we didn't care. My father was supposed to be paying Mum a regular sum every week but often he didn't bother. My brothers and I were frequently despatched to his office to collect some cash, but he'd keep us waiting all day and then maybe hand us five pounds. Not expecting to be there so long, we seldom brought lunch and the men at the warehouse felt so sorry for us they often gave us their own sandwiches. Sometimes my father didn't even turn up at all and the men gave us our bus fare home.

Mum did the best she could but often there was very little food. She made big bread and butter puddings with the raisins eked out sparingly and we ate a lot of eggs, which were cheap, though they had to be poached because there was no oil left in which to fry them. Then the electricity and the gas were cut off because she couldn't pay the bills so she filled the house with candles and borrowed a camping stove for cooking.

Gary made expeditions down to the pier at the Mumbles with his fishing rod to try to catch mackerel for our tea. He was often surprisingly successful, but even so there were days when there was no food. I remember once rummaging through the pantry looking for something, anything, I could eat. All I could find was a jar of jam and a tin of condensed milk. Delicious, they were.

Another day Debbie told me that we were going to

have a square meal for a change and then she gave me an Oxo cube. That was our dinner. She thought it was a great joke. And I laughed too because, although we were hungry, we were still so relieved not to have to worry about my father coming home, it seemed a small price to pay.

Sometimes the aunties would arrive with wonderful bags of food, and clothes that our cousins had outgrown. Debbie and I were overjoyed to see them but Mum received their largesse with a small unconvincing smile. She was a proud woman and, grateful as she was for their generosity, she hated having to accept such gifts. She'd been the lady in the big house with diamonds and furs, the woman strangers used to envy. Now she was reduced to hand-outs.

It was obvious we couldn't go on like that, and eventually Mum managed to get a job cooking in a café in the centre of town. We loved it.

'Come down for tea after school,' she'd say. And we'd pile into the steamy café, dropping our school bags on the formica chairs, to feast on fish, chips and beans followed by pancakes and maple syrup.

'Take it out my wages, Phil,' Mum would say to Phil Cobley, the kindly owner, as she watched us eat, but I don't suppose he did.

We couldn't do that every evening, of course, but when we didn't eat at the café Mum would collect up the day's uneaten chips and bring them back for our supper. It's surprising how good cold chips can be.

After a while, though, we noticed a change in Mum.

She'd pop into the garden to hang out the washing, a scarf tied over the rollers in her hair, then a man would walk by and wave. Mum would drop the washing, run in, rip off her scarf, pull out the rollers, slash some lipstick across her mouth and be back outside returning his wave in thirty seconds flat.

What a way for a mature woman of 36 to behave, Debbie and I remarked to each other disapprovingly.

But we began to see a lot of Don, as we eventually discovered Mum's admirer was called. He was an easy-going man with a droopy moustache and a nervous smile. He took to calling in of an evening to play cards with us, and since he always came armed with a bottle of pop, several bags of crisps and some sweets, he was a welcome visitor.

Then one day the postman pushed some letters through the door and Mum opened one and started to cry. It was from the bank. The manager was writing to inform her that our father was in financial difficulties. He'd re-mortgaged the house, hadn't made sufficient payments and now we would have to leave.

At around the same time, Don discovered the reason we had so many candles about the house was not due to Mum's artistic nature but because the electricity had been cut off. Appalled, he decided we should all move in with him. Since we were on the verge of becoming homeless, we were very glad to be offered a roof over our heads and central heating that worked, too!

Don seemed to us to be a knight in shining armour. He lived in a comfortable house in a different part of

Swansea and he was a welder. We liked him. He was gentle and softly spoken and he made me a pair of metal stilts which was amazing. I taught myself to walk on them and I was the only person in the whole street who could walk like a circus performer. But the only drawback to living with Don was that I had to change schools.

School life hadn't always been easy for me. Over the years the teachers had wondered what to do with me. I was intelligent enough, they said, but for some reason I had a difficulty with reading. I so wanted to read. At one point my cousin Julie used to sit next to me in class and she'd sail through a book without faltering, but when I looked at the words she could decipher with such ease, they might as well have been written in Chinese. No matter how I stared at them they wouldn't reveal their meaning. How I envied Julie.

Back home I'd tearfully ask Mum, 'Why can't I read? I want to read!' And she'd sit there with me for hours, patiently going over and over my book, breaking each word into syllables and sounding it out for me. But I couldn't grasp it. We'd never heard of dyslexia in those days, so I just felt stupid.

The school was very good, though. They gave me extra reading and writing lessons and got me to write the word 'Bed' at the top of every page of my exercise book.

'Imagine lying on a bed with a "b" at the top and a "d" by your feet,' Mrs Jones the teacher would remind me, and it helped.

It also helped that they gave me the passages I had to

read aloud in class well in advance so that I could 'practise' at home. In fact, practising didn't make much difference, so I just memorised the whole thing and recited it the next day as if I was reading. I did the same with my spellings and with my French, and in this way I managed quite well.

Unfortunately my new school was not so enlightened. It was a rougher place. The children referred to their mothers as 'mam' whereas we'd been taught to say 'mum' and they were allowed to say 'thanks' where my old school insisted on 'thank you'. The children probably thought I was posh and the teachers weren't all as caring as they might have been.

I was horrified to notice that one of the lads in the English class couldn't cope with his work and sat there playing with paperclips throughout the lesson. Instead of offering help, the next day the teacher gave him a big handful of paperclips and left him to it. I could see that I was going to get very little support in this place and I lost interest.

It wasn't much better in the playground. My best friend Becky's mum was having problems with her memory and one day Jackie, the school bully, found out about it. Immediately she started picking on Becky.

'Your mam's mental,' she taunted. 'Doo-lally she is, your mam.'

And she began dribbling her fingers up and down over her lips making insulting, idiot sounds.

'That's how your mam talks, isn't it? That's your mam that is.'

Becky looked upset. She bit her lip and turned away, but I was furious.

'Don't you talk about her mum like that!' I shouted, confronting Jackie angrily. 'She's better than your mum anyway. 'Least she taught her daughter manners.'

'Ooooooh listen to the Queen! Muuum! Muuum, is it?' mimicked Jackie. 'Why don't you talk like everyone else?'

And she reached out and grabbed my hair, dragging me towards her.

'I'm going to have you, I am!'

At that point a passing teacher saw what was going on and came and pulled her away, but Jackie was not prepared to apologise.

'You wait,' she sneered over her shoulder as she was led back to the school. 'I'm going to have you tomorrow. For certain. You wait.'

My stomach did a triple somersault. Speaking up for myself was one thing, fighting quite another. I'd seen some of the school fights. At the first hint of trouble word would spread, apparently by telepathy, and in an instant a big crowd would form around the combatants. The audience would divide into two rowdy teams, each loudly urging their champion on.

Jackie was much bigger than I and a real tomboy; I had no doubt I'd be thrashed and humiliated in front of the whole school.

That night I couldn't sleep. I prayed and prayed. I didn't want to fight and I begged for help. The Lined Man had not been visiting so often since my father left, but as I began to whisper my anguished pleas he appeared beside my bed.

'It's all right. Don't worry. It'll be fine,' he reassured me the way he always did. 'I'm with you.'

But unless he could arrange a crash course in karate I didn't see what he could do.

The next day Mum, who was a great believer in getting an education, refused to let me stay at home. She was not impressed by claims of headaches, stomach aches or feeling sick.

'You'll feel better when you get to school,' she insisted as she packed me off. I didn't want to tell her the truth because I didn't want to worry her.

I crept along, dragging my feet and staring around, expecting an avenging Jackie to leap out at me at any second. But nothing happened. There was no sign of her on the way to school.

All morning I couldn't concentrate on my lessons and at lunchtime my stomach was churning so much I couldn't eat a thing. Yet there was still no sign of Jackie. Where could she be? I knew she enjoyed a scrap and that she would be looking forward to our encounter as much as I was dreading it.

It wasn't until we were leaving to go home that one of her classmates finally found me.

'Have you heard about Jackie?' she asked.

'No,' I replied, trying to slide away before she could run and tell Jackie where I was.

'She got knocked down this morning!'

'No!' I cried, feeling a pang of guilt. 'She's not . . .'

'No, she's going to be okay,' said the friend. 'She's just bruised and shaken up. She got off the bus on the way to school and was crossing the road when this car came round the corner and hit her. Lucky for you, huh?'

I was speechless. Relief turned my knees to jelly and a picture jumped into my head. There was a big red bus nosing through the morning traffic and as I watched, Jackie in her school uniform, bag swinging, pushed down the step and hopped out into the road without looking. The car behind tried to swerve around her but just clipped the edge of her school bag and sent her spinning across the tarmac.

I blinked.

'Are you okay, Di?' Becky was saying. 'Serves her right eh?'

I grinned.

'Yes, serves her right.' But I couldn't help feeling guilty all the same. Was it my fault, or was I crazy to even think like that?

Fortunately Jackie made a full recovery, but by the time she came back to school she seemed to have forgotten about our disagreement. She gave me no bother after that. In fact it might have been my imagination, but she seemed to steer clear of me from then on.

As the months passed by, my friends, like most young girls, started day-dreaming about the future and who they would marry. They developed a powerful interest in fortune-telling and for some reason formed the idea that the local spiritualist church might help them tap into the supernatural. They talked me into going with them to the services, where we'd sit at the back and giggle at the various mediums who came onto the stage. It was just a bit of fun to us then. Many of the mediums seemed old and a bit dowdy to us teenagers whispering annoyingly in the last row, a chattering huddle of mini-skirts, extravagant eye-shadow and feather ear-rings. Not surprisingly, none of us received a message from the spirit world, but I was secretly fascinated by the way those mediums worked and one day one of them suddenly pointed at me and said, 'I can see you look as if you've got your own little army of spirit people behind you!' This couldn't be proved either way, of course, and my friends found it hysterically funny, but knowing what I already knew about the Lined Man and my spirit sisters and brothers who still dropped in to say hello from time to time, I could quite believe it.

Some of the mediums seemed to have a genuine power, but others gave me the impression they were making the whole thing up. Was this business a load of rubbish, or could there be something more to it? Despite all my conversations with the Lined Man I could see no connection between his quiet private visits, in which we had proper conversations, and the cryptic messages relayed to the audience from that scuffed platform.

Looking back, it was very naughty of us not to be more respectful, but we didn't understand that this was a religion, taken just as seriously by its followers as my mother's Catholic faith.

But, undeterred by their lack of encouragement from the other side, my friends continued to explore. One night I came home from school to find Debbie and her friend Michaela huddled round a Ouija board. It was only a game, I told myself, but there was something about it that made the hairs on the back of my neck prickle.

I sat down to watch just as Debbie asked loudly and slowly, as if she expected the spirits to be a bit deaf: 'WHO-AM-I-GOING-TO-MARRY?'

The glass seemed to spin round the board, dragging the girls' fingers with it and moved towards the letter S and then to the letter R – which made us think of the toothpaste Mum often bought.

'You'll marry a man called Stephen,' I said without thinking.

Debbie glared at me for interrupting. 'We'll see,' she said. 'Right. S.R! Could be Simon, could be Sean, could be Stephen, I suppose . . .'

And they continued with their queries to the unknown spirit apparently trapped in Don's old tumbler. I didn't think much of the game, yet, oddly enough, a few years later Debbie did indeed marry a man called Stephen. Stephen Radford. S. R.

Another night I went to my friend Joanne's for tea. Joanne's mum was divorced like ours and appeared to be quite content with her peaceful single state. Yet as I stood there sipping orange squash a sudden picture popped into my head of Joanne's mum hand in hand with a nice looking man with dark hair and dark eyes.

There was something about the closeness between them that made me think they were getting married.

'D'you know what?' I heard myself say to Joanne. 'Your mum's going to meet a man with dark eyes and brown hair and she's going to end up marrying him.'

Joanne gave me a wary look. 'I don't think so,' she said.

But a few weeks later her mum unexpectedly met a man who looked just as I'd described. They hit it off instantly, there was a whirlwind romance and it wasn't long before they were married.

After that I began to develop a bit of a reputation. My friends started asking me questions to see what I'd say.

'Am I going to meet a new boy tonight?' (Sometimes yes, sometimes no.)

'Is my boyfriend two-timing me?' (Usually, yes.)

'Here Diane, see if you can do that thing where you pick up vibes from people's stuff,' and they'd hand me a ring, or a watch or some personal item. This sounded like nonsense to me but when I ran the object through my fingers, quite often it would seem to come alive in my hand. It tingled against my skin and sent strange pictures to my mind. When I described the images to the owner of the trinket, she often claimed to know exactly what I was talking about.

This odd knack that I seemed to possess puzzled me as much as it puzzled them. It didn't seem to resemble the powers of the mediums at the spiritualist church, but it was obviously something a bit out of the ordinary. Quite often I thought the things I was saying were guesses, but it was uncanny how many of my guesses turned out to be right. Maybe I was 'psychic' as my friends clearly thought, though I didn't really know what that word meant. I would go round and round in circles trying to understand it and then give up. It was just the way I was. When I thought of it at all, I regarded my 'gift' as a sort of party game. Yet it wasn't always as harmless as it appeared.

One evening at a friend's party, I was holding a bracelet belonging to a girl a little older than me who I'd never met before and I said, 'D'you know why you lost that baby?' Her face turned strangely pale but, lost in my mental pictures, I scarcely noticed.

'No,' she whispered.

I wasn't seeing the girl or her bracelet; in front of my eyes was a tiny little scrap with a misshapen head and oddly twisted features. The poor baby seemed to move painfully towards me and then suddenly it smiled, turned back and disappeared into a bright white light that came streaming from somewhere behind.

'There was something wrong with it,' I said matter-of-factly, handing back the bracelet. 'It was damaged. That's why it couldn't be born.'

The girl gave an odd little stifled cry, dropped the bracelet and ran out of the room.

I looked round at the ring of startled faces staring blankly up at me. None of us had even known she was pregnant but now the poor girl was sobbing her heart out in the bathroom and it was my fault.

I felt dreadful. It had never seriously crossed my

mind before that I could upset people with the things I said. Until that moment I was accustomed to my strange remarks being treated either with exasperation on the part of my family; disbelief, since often the accuracy of my statements couldn't be confirmed until a later date; or, more recently, fascination. My friends were getting used to the idea that I could give them interesting little predictions about boyfriends and romance and increasingly they were pleading with me to entertain them.

Like most teenagers I was a little unsure of myself, still discovering who I was, and it was nice to be popular. Who wouldn't like being in demand? But I didn't really think of my ability as a talent I could use at will. I didn't particularly trust it to work whenever I called upon it and I was as astonished as everyone else when something I'd predicted actually happened. 'Unbelievable!' I'd marvel when someone mentioned later that they'd met the boy I'd told them they'd date, or that the car I'd said they'd own had suddenly materialised in their life.

'How do you do it, Di?' they'd ask.

'I have no idea,' I'd tell them. They didn't believe me, but it was true. Sometimes I said the first thing that came into my head, sometimes I heard a voice mention a name, sometimes I'd see a little picture. Where this information came from I couldn't even guess and I had no way of knowing whether it was relevant or not. All I did was pass it on in a light-hearted way. I didn't even use it for myself. It didn't seem necessary. Whenever I needed any help I could call the Lined Man and somehow things would work out – just as they had with Jackie the school bully.

So, until I met the girl with the miscarried baby, my uncanny powers were no more than a game to me, and then suddenly I was confronted by the reality of what I was doing. I was seeing into the truth of other people's lives – the bad as well as the good – and they only wanted to hear the good.

Although I didn't know it then, the look that crossed that girl's face as I described the worst moment of her life was a look that was to haunt me again and again over the years. A kind of horror, a backing away.

She'd asked me to tell her what I saw but when I did, it was almost as if she blamed me for seeing something unpleasant. I think I was almost as shocked as she was. I made up my mind there and then never again to be so blunt unless someone asked me specifically to tell them the whole story, warts and all.

I was glad to get home that night. I wanted to come back down to earth. Nothing was so pleasing as the sight of Mum standing at the ironing board, busily squashing every crease out of her work trousers while Don made a cup of tea in the kitchen. Mum and Don had no truck with psychic nonsense. Mum half believed, I suspected, but she was so worried that people might think I was crazy she tried to shut me up whenever I mentioned anything strange. As for Don, he was a typical 'when you're dead, you're dead' sceptic.

Yet I didn't mind at all. The best thing about coming

home was feeling normal again. Thanks to Don we were a family once more, which was comforting, and we even had the granny that Debbie and I had always craved – Don's mother Gladys.

Gladys was lovely. A proper grey-haired old lady with poor arthritic, twisted hands and a shuffle when she walked, but even though she wasn't in the best of health she was a wonderful woman with a great sense of humour.

I loved Gladys and I went to visit her as often as I could. She lived a few miles across town and when Don wasn't able to run me there in the car I used to get out my roller skates and slog all the way on my own, even though it took about three hours. Gladys would be waiting in the kitchen, comfortably ensconced in her big wooden chair beside the Rayburn stove. She wouldn't be without her Rayburn, Gladys used to say. Every night in the winter she put a brick into the oven and then took it up with her to warm her bed.

Gladys might have been in her seventies but she was a good sport. She let me play hairdressers with her springy grey curls and I'd brush them and brush them and then divide them into dozens of tiny pony tails all over her head. She sat there bristling with rubber bands like an elderly punk and we laughed and laughed until we couldn't speak and our sides hurt.

When I was about 14, Gladys caught pneumonia. Things looked pretty serious for a while but then she seemed to recover and went to stay with Don's sister Beryl to recuperate. I was looking forward to the day that Gladys would be well enough to return to her own home and I could skate over for another hairdressing session. Then early one Sunday evening, not long after Gladys had gone to Beryl's, I dozed off over my homework and had a strange dream. Gladys was standing in front of me smiling and she was proudly showing me a mass of beautiful pink carnations. Beside her was a man with receding hair and a smile exactly like Don's. Once the man was sure I'd admired the flowers, he beckoned Gladys away with his hand. Gladys gave me one last smile and followed him.

I jumped and woke suddenly to hear Mum coming up to bed.

'Mum!' I called softly. 'Gran's going to die.'

A sigh floated in from the landing. 'Oh Diane,' said Mum, 'Aren't you old enough now not to come out with all this strange talk? Gran's fine. She's better now.'

'No, I saw a man coming to get her,' I said. 'It's going to happen next week.' And as I was speaking I heard the word 'Monday' in the back of my mind. 'Next Monday in fact,' I added.

'Diane I'm tired . . .' Mum began, and then Don's voice called out from downstairs.

'Are you in the bathroom, Pat?'

'On my way!' Mum called back. 'Goodnight love,' she said to me and then hurried away.

I didn't know what to make of it. Deep down I knew I was right but I didn't want to believe it. I loved Gladys and I wanted to believe she was better. It was only a dream, I tried to tell myself.

But the following Monday, Gladys passed away peacefully in her sleep. Mum was shocked. Obviously my prediction could have been nothing more than a coincidence and that's what she preferred to believe, yet inside I think she knew differently. Still, her main concern was that people would not understand if I came out with anything 'strange' and might take against me. She wanted me to be normal at all costs. 'Just don't say anything to Don – or the relatives,' she warned me.

I didn't attend the funeral service itself as I was considered too young, but I'm told the church was awash with pink carnations. And afterwards some relatives who'd not seen him for some time remarked to Don how much like his late father he was becoming, except of course that his father had been going bald.

Chapter Seven

Becky and I were really excited. We were off for our first night out on our own as young women, well, seventeen-year-olds. We were going to a club. Though, to be honest it wasn't so much a club as the upstairs of a pub, and a pub that was a bit on the rough side at that – but the upstairs had been redesigned and been given a sophisticated name of its own: 'Shades'. It sounded so much more glamorous than The Prince of Wales. There was music and dancing, and my friend Becky and I had bought brand new outfits to mark the occasion.

As good friends often do, we'd dressed ourselves like sisters in identical outfits but of different colours. I was a vision in burgundy, at least that was the effect I was after. I put on a burgundy pin-striped skirt, pink blouse trimmed with burgundy ribbon, burgundy blazer and burgundy leather boots, while Becky wore the same only in blue. Didn't we look good, we told each other happily.

While Becky zipped up her blue boots I went over to the mirror to finish brushing my hair. It was newly washed and a bit fly-away and it needed some vigorous grooming to get it to shine. But as I leant forward to check my reflection there seemed to be something wrong with the mirror. It was misty somehow. Thinking it must have steamed up I grabbed a handful of tissues and wiped it, but it made no difference.

'Stupid mirror,' I said crossly. 'It's gone all cloudy. I can hardly see myself.'

'Your hair looks fine!' said Becky, standing up and taking a few experimental steps in her new boots. 'Come on, we'll have to hurry or we'll miss the bus.'

I glanced back at the mirror, slightly troubled. There was something not right about that glass. It was dry to the touch and yet it looked as if it was full of cloud. I'd never seen anything like it.

'It looks like a mirror to me,' said Becky picking up her handbag. 'Come on. It's nearly half-past.'

I took one last look at the mirror. Something bad's going to happen tonight, I thought fleetingly, but then Becky was clattering out of the door and I hurried to follow her. The next minute the pair of us were off into the Swansea evening, dressed to impress.

'Shades' was everything we'd hoped for. Crowded, lively, with spinning lights and Meatloaf pulsing so loudly the floor vibrated. Becky and I stood there clutching our orange juices trying to look cool. We loved the music and I was enjoying myself, but I couldn't get rid of this edgy feeling. I hung about on the fringes of the room continually looking round for the source of danger. Yet everything seemed completely normal.

The music got louder, the room hotter and nothing happened. Becky and I danced round our handbags and shouted conversation into each other's ear, yet inside I was getting more and more strung up.

Then, suddenly, a picture of blue tattoos on a meaty pink arm passed before my eyes. I glanced round to see a girl in dungarees moving towards us through the crowd. Her arms were bare and she had tattoos from shoulder to elbow, but before I had time to wonder if these were the same tattoos I'd just seen, one arm lifted and something was skimming through the air.

I heard a tinkle of breaking glass and my lip felt wet. Puzzled, I put my hand up to my mouth and my fingers came away red with blood.

'Oh, Di!' cried Becky in horror. 'You're bleeding!'

The crowd parted around us, bouncers converged on the girl in dungarees and Becky was frantically pulling tissues out of her bag to press to my lip.

I hadn't seen it coming but the girl, apparently having finished her drink, just threw the glass across the dance floor. It flew over our heads, hit a pillar and smashed, and one of the pieces bounced back and cut my face.

Blood was pouring all down my lovely new pink blouse as the police arrived. I didn't see what happened to the girl in dungarees, I don't even know if she intended to attack me, but I was taken to hospital where three stitches were put into my by now immensely swollen lip.

Mum was distraught at the state of me when I got home; so was Debbie; but although it stung quite a bit, I was more upset about my ruined blouse and the disappointing end to my first grown-up evening.

Without thinking I went upstairs to inspect the damage in the mirror. My reflection gleamed back at me, swollen and blood-stained but crystal clear. The fuzzy cloud had completely evaporated.

It was a warning, I realised. But it was a warning I would continue to ignore.

I was still struggling to understand the strange abilities I seemed to have. I felt completely normal yet I saw things and heard things that other people obviously didn't and I didn't know why. Why should I be able to do things they couldn't? In every other way I was no different from anyone else.

Everyone was still in the grip of the Ouija board craze and one day I came home to find Debbie and her old friend Michaela bent over the now familiar board, watching the glass avidly. But my stomach started to churn as I looked at them because standing over the table with a disapproving look on his face was the Lined Man, who still visited me regularly. By now I trusted him implicitly and regarded him as a sort of guardian angel.

'Oh, hello Di,' said Debbie, looking up. 'D'you want to come and join in?'

I was about to say yes when I saw that the Lined Man was frowning at me. He shook his head in a way that couldn't be misinterpreted.

As usual, neither Debbie nor Michaela seemed to be aware of him. And I hurried away.

I wanted answers but I didn't know where to find them, until one day after school I was helping Mum at the café when I heard some women talking about a well-known psychic who lived a few miles away on the other side of Neath.

'Incredible he was,' one woman was telling the other, 'unbelievable. The things he told me. He couldn't possibly have known.'

I took my cloth and started wiping a table just behind them.

'I've heard of that Danny Lester before,' said the other woman. 'They say he's good, but you never know do you?'

'Good? He told me things no-one knew. Even my husband didn't know.'

'Never! D'you think he might see me?'

'Oh, I expect so,' said the first woman. 'You have to make an appointment, mind, but he's in the phone book.'

'Are you going to be all night with that table, Diane?' Mum's voice cut in sharply from across the café. 'There'll be more customers along in a minute.'

My wiping went into overdrive. 'Just finished,' I said and I scurried off to get the cutlery.

The next day I couldn't wait to get to school to tell Julie. Julie, my clever cousin who could read so well, was now a bubbly blonde with an intense curiosity about the unexplained. She'd grown used to my knack of making amazingly accurate guesses over the years and she accepted my 'psychic powers' quite matter-of-factly. I think she even believed in them more than I did. I knew that she'd be as eager as I was to meet this Danny Lester.

We looked up his number in the phone book and I made a nervous call, half expecting to be told not to be so silly and that the great man didn't see schoolgirls. But the woman who answered was very kind. She made no comment about the youthfulness of our voices, gave us an appointment for 6 pm the following Tuesday and explained how we should find the house.

Julie and I were thrilled. Julie emptied every coin from her money box and I collected my wages from Phil, who paid me £11 a week to wipe tables at the café at weekends and after school.

When Tuesday arrived Julie and I caught two buses from Swansea and then walked quite a distance out into the countryside until we came to a large cottage sur-rounded by fields. Despite a sudden attack of nerves, we dared each other to walk up the path and knock on the door. The buses had been slow so we were late and by now we were half hoping we'd be turned away.

But not a bit of it. 'Don't worry, dears,' said the plump middle-aged woman who answered the door. She was wearing a big apron and she looked as if she'd been cooking all day. 'Danny's running late. Come in and have a seat.' And she led us into a faded room with floral wallpaper and a flowered sofa with exhausted springs. When we sat down we sank right through the cushions almost to the floor. A great deal of antique-looking china stood around and Danny seemed to have a penchant for jug and bowl sets.

'Just a normal house then,' said Julie. 'He must keep all his crystal balls upstairs!'

'I wonder if he'll be wearing a turban?' I joked and we started to giggle, but just then a woman came hurrying from the next room crying, her head down, and rushed out of the door. I turned to Julie in alarm but before we could make a bolt for it too, a man's voice called: 'Next please!' And the plump woman in the apron was ushering me in to see Danny.

To my disappointment I found myself in another ordinary room. There was not a crystal ball to be seen and Danny was not even wearing a turban. In fact he was a bit younger than I'd been expecting and dressed unremarkably in a blue shirt. He could have been a teacher.

'Well, my girl. You've been seeing spirits from a very early age, haven't you?' he said as soon as I sat down. 'Do you realise that you'll be doing this when you're older?'

I stared at him silently.

'You can read anything,' he went on. 'In fact, you'll be famous one day. You will drive a black car and your grandad's helping you. William is with you too. And your mother's a very good cook.'

I wasn't greatly impressed. It's easy to tell a young person they'll be famous one day and, much as I would have liked to believe him, I couldn't see how that would happen. I didn't know anyone called William and though my mum was a good cook, didn't everyone think that about their mother? It was funny how he knew I saw spirits though.

Julie was more satisfied with her own reading. She

was told she would grow up to marry a man called Stephen. Which is exactly what happened in the following years.

When I got home I told Mum all about it over dinner.

'Of course you know of a William,' she said when I'd finished 'That was my father's name. Your other grandad.'

I was stunned.

'Huh,' said Don, cutting into a potato, 'waste of money if you ask me.'

He absolutely refused to believe any such nonsense, no matter what evidence was presented to him. Even if Gladys herself had walked in and handed him another slice of pie he would have thought he was hallucinating. Mum, on the other hand, was much more receptive. She was willing to accept there might be something in it when other people claimed to be psychic. She just didn't want me going down that controversial route myself.

I didn't know what to make of it, but the experience gave me a little more confidence to experiment and to play a few pranks. One night I was out with my sister, Debbie, and we had put on our smart black dresses and gone to a proper nightclub in Swansea. We were chatting and sipping drinks when a smart young man in a crisp white shirt and dark trousers came and plonked himself down beside me.

'Use your psychic powers, Diane!' Debbie whispered to me. 'Tell me what he's thinking. Read his palm!'

The young man raised his eyebrows enquiringly. He couldn't hear what Debbie said but he was curious.

'My sister can read palms,' said Debbie mischievously.

'Oh, can she?' said the young man with a smile. 'Well have a little look at mine then. I'd like to buy you girls a drink.'

'Let's see your palm first,' I said and I pretended to examine the square, nicely-manicured hand placed in mine.

'You've been away for some time then,' I said.

He stared at me, his face expressionless. 'What d'you mean by that?'

'You and I both know that you've been away,' I repeated.

'Yeah, I've been abroad,' he said, his voice very cool.

But I could see bars in front of his face and the Lined Man was showing me the 'get out of jail' card from a Monopoly set.

'No, you've not been abroad,' I said. 'You've been in prison.'

His face went completely white. He wrenched his hand out of mine and jumped up. 'I think I'd better leave,' he said.

'Okay,' I said brightly. 'Bye!'

Debbie watched him go in amazement.

'Did you really see that?' she asked.

'Yes I did,' I said.

'How?'

And I explained about the bars and the jail symbol.

'Amazing,' said Debbie, but I still don't think she totally believed it was anything more than a lucky stab in the dark.

These things were just a bit of fun. Danny Lester's prediction that somehow I would end up making this line of work my career seemed so unlikely I never even considered it. The problem was, what could I do? I'd lost all confidence at school and couldn't face taking my GCSEs. What was the point? I was bound to fail because no matter how much I knew, my dyslexia made it take me too long to read and write the papers. I ran out of time before I was anywhere near finished. With no qualifications college was out, so I'd have to get a job.

'You've always liked helping me in the kitchen,' said Mum. 'Why don't you look for a cooking job? You won't need any qualifications for that.'

It was true I did like cooking, but when I thought of how tired Mum was when she came home night after night from the café, and the hours she spent peeling great piles of potatoes, I didn't think I wanted that for myself. If I could choose, I'd prefer something that wasn't such hard work.

'I do like cooking,' I said tactfully, 'but really I'd prefer my own place.'

'Well, you want to go into management then,' said Mum, 'but you'll need qualifications for that unless you work your way up. Why not start off in the kitchen and you can see what happens.'

I was still thinking it over when an odd thing happened. Late one afternoon there was a strange little tap on the door-knocker, an envelope fell through the letter box onto the mat, and I glanced out the window in time to see a nurse hurrying away down the road.

'What on earth . . .?' I thought in surprise, bending down to pick up the envelope, and then I was even more surprised to see my own name printed in hurried capitals, staring back at me.

Inside was a short note: 'Dear Miss Preston, Your father has asked me to inform you that he is currently a patient at Singleton Hospital. He is very poorly and he would like to see you. I do hope you will be able to look in during visiting hours . . .'

I was stunned. I hadn't seen or heard from my father since we went to live at Don's several years ago. Mum had an idea that after our old house was sold he'd gone to Spain to open a bar. What was he doing back in Wales and what could be wrong with him?

Just the very words 'your father' made my stomach turn over. I never thought about him any more. I didn't want to. I hoped to erase his memory from my mind completely. I hadn't realised when he was still living with us how deeply he affected me, but now I was free of him I wanted to keep it that way.

I won't go, I thought to myself. I don't care what's wrong with him. I won't go. But, to my surprise, when I told Mum she didn't agree.

'And it's only you he wants to see?' she queried. 'Not Debbie or the boys?'

'It doesn't mention them in the letter,' I said.

Mum tapped her lip. 'Hmmmm. I wonder what's wrong with the old devil?'

'I don't know and I don't care,' I said. 'And I'm surprised you're interested.'

Mum blushed slightly. 'Well, after all these years . . .
I don't care exactly . . . But I'd like to know.'

'Well, you go then. I'm not!'

'Diane!' said Mum. 'How can I go? He's not asking for
me. It's you he wants to see and I think you should go.
If you don't, you'll be sorry. He is your father after all.'

I was dead against it at first but eventually she talked
me round. I was terrified of seeing him again and
determined not to go alone. Mum couldn't come with
me, of course, so instead I asked my cousin Julie. Julie
was always up for anything.

'Don't be scared,' said Julie sensibly. 'What can he do
to you in hospital? You'll be quite safe.'

But her words didn't comfort me; I remained scared.
I was also gripped with horror at the idea of him seeing
me suddenly grown into a woman. It was about five
years since he'd last set eyes on me and back then I was
a small, flat-chested little girl. I was quite different now
and I only had myself to blame.

Walking on the beach one day with two friends
when I was about 15, I couldn't help noticing how
they'd developed proper curves while I was still flat as
a pancake. So I started praying for boobs. I think I
overdid it. I prayed so much that eventually I developed boobs of more generous proportions than I had in
mind. And now I couldn't bear the thought of my
father noticing. Desperately embarrassed, I swathed
myself in a big loose coat before Julie and I set off for
the hospital.

My feet dragged as I made them walk reluctantly up

through the beds of the men's ward and my heart was thumping painfully. I didn't know what I was afraid of, because it was obvious that my father couldn't turn violent in a place like this, and yet, fear grabbed me round the throat.

When I reached the bed of my father I hardly recognised him: he seemed to have shrunk and was much smaller than I remembered. I found myself staring at this weak, thin-looking man in striped pyjamas, with sallow skin and grey streaks in his dull black hair. He was lying back on his pillows yelping in pain.

Apparently, when in Spain, he'd developed some sort of abscess on his leg that wouldn't heal properly. He'd ended up having an operation and a blood transfusion and there was a problem with clotting. He came back to Wales but gangrene set in and he'd had to have two toes amputated.

It was a sad story but I found myself unmoved. All the time he was talking I was looking at him thinking, what do I feel? I don't feel anything. I don't feel any more pity than I'd feel for a complete stranger in a similar situation. You're a stranger to me.

'So, Diane,' he said after while. 'You're going to give up school. Well, if you must leave, how would you like to go to Spain and run my business for me? I've got a bar out there called Taffy's Bar in Magaluf. You'd like Magaluf. You always did like the sun, didn't you? There are some apartments too. While I'm laid up here I need someone I can trust to take care of it all.'

My face felt as if it was frozen. 'I want to go into hotel management,' I heard myself say stiffly.

'Well that would be ideal,' said my father. 'Perfect training for hotel management my bar would be.'

But before I could answer I was aware of two new figures hurrying down the ward. There was a big lady in a baggy grey jumper with dark greasy hair and a little boy, a lovely child with big brown eyes and dark hair. The pair of them stopped beside my father's bed.

'Diane, this is my wife Magda,' said my father coolly.

Magda treated me to a dagger glance while I stared in shock at her chunky figure and ungroomed appearance. How could he possibly prefer this untidy creature to my pretty, vivacious mum?

'I was just saying to Diane that she should manage Taffy's for me,' said my father to his new wife.

Magda's gaze became even frostier. She was livid, I could tell, but she made no comment.

'Well, I haven't made up my mind yet,' I mumbled, anxious to get out of there.

'But this would be ideal, Diane. Ideal,' my father insisted, while at his side Magda assured me silently that it was the last thing I should ever contemplate if I knew what was good for me.

'Anyway, I must go,' I said. 'Julie's waiting.'

And before he could protest I backed away from the bedside and dashed for the swing doors.

'You'll look in again, won't you . . . ?' came my father's voice from across the beds.

I gave a vague wave of my hand that might have been

yes, might have been no and the doors crashed shut behind me.

'Look at your face!' said Julie as I bolted round the corner. 'What happened!'

And I had to go through it all again. And then again when I got home to Mum.

It was an unsettling episode and I didn't want to think about it. I certainly didn't intend to go back. I felt nothing for my father, I realised. It was as if I didn't have a father. Yet this was a troubling thought: no matter what he'd done, he was still family. Wasn't it wicked to feel nothing for your father at all? I couldn't answer these questions and so, rather than agonise over the subject, I threw myself into my new career.

Well, I say career but I suppose it wasn't a career in the conventional sense. I'd been talking to my friend Cheryl who worked in the Dickens coffee shop across the road from the Grand Theatre and she mentioned that all sorts of celebrities dropped in for a snack after the show. This sounded exciting. Much more exciting than Phil's café, and I thought that if I was going to go into catering then somewhere like the Dickens would be the most interesting place to start. They were look-ing for evening staff, Cheryl told me. 'Oh, do apply Di!' she said. 'It'll be great with the two of us,' and before I knew it I was working evenings at the Dickens.

The coffee shop was housed in a very old black-and-white timbered building that leaned in an exhausted way against the place next door. The roof tilted side-ways and the floors slanted and Cheryl and I used to move with a list as we scurried about. Although the Dickens called itself a coffee shop it was actually a bistro which served meals, and Robert, the owner, decided to teach Cheryl and me how to cook. I particularly enjoyed discovering the secret of perfect lasagne – a dish I'd never seen assembled before. Over the weeks I learned a heck of a lot and it wasn't long before I could concoct any number of starters and I mastered several quick ways with an omelette. I did draw the line at frogs' legs, though. The very idea of them made me feel sick!

We were getting on so well that some evenings Cheryl and I would be left in charge and I'd stare out across the checked tablecloths at the happy diners and pretend I was in my own little restaurant. The only problem with such an old building as the Dickens was that it was rather spooky upstairs and I frequently saw the hazy outline of an elderly woman wandering around when I had to go up there to fetch something. I called her Marjorie, though she never told me her name. But the hairs on the back of my neck always stood up in an unpleasant way when I went to the upper floor, and it felt as if she didn't want anybody else in what she regarded as her territory. I tried to avoid going there if I could help it.

The Dickens only needed me in the evenings, but there was no way Mum wanted me hanging round the house all day, so I took a day-time job as a kitchen assistant at Peter Jones, a big cafeteria in town.

It was an interesting experience but I didn't enjoy the

work as much as I did at the laid-back coffee house. Peter Jones was more formal and we had to wear blue overalls and little blue hats which I didn't much like. Also, one of the older women in the kitchen seemed to take a dislike to me.

I don't know why, but she went out of her way to make cutting comments, and if ever I was sent to fetch something from the big walk-in freezer she'd invariably shut the door on me.

'Oh, sorry!' she'd exclaim in mock-horror when someone eventually let me out, chilled to the bone, 'Didn't realise you were in there. I thought someone had left the door open.'

I got quite depressed working in that atmosphere but I learned a lot about catering and it stood me in good stead later on.

It was a learning experience in a different way, too. One afternoon there was a commotion downstairs and we heard an ambulance siren wailing up the road.

'There's a man on the ground floor might have had a heart attack!' said one of the waitresses, rushing into the kitchen for a glass of water.

I shouldn't have left my post, of course, but I was bored and I couldn't resist going to find out what was happening. 'I'll just see if anyone needs some tea!' I called over my shoulder as I scrambled away downstairs before they could stop me.

I reached the ground floor just in time to see two ambulancemen lifting a motionless figure out of a chair and laying him onto a stretcher. The poor man had collapsed just as he'd been served his faggots and peas. He didn't even have time to take a bite. Worried shoppers and staff were clustered round but the ambulancemen motioned them back. They bent over the man and rechecked his heart and his pulse. Then they unrolled a blanket and pulled it up, right over his face.

He must be dead! I thought to myself, shocked. I'd never seen a dead body before. But then I glanced up from the stretcher and saw that, far from being dead, the man had managed to stand himself up and was walking round in front of the chair, right as rain. Yet the ambulancemen hadn't noticed this and they began to carry the stretcher out to the waiting vehicle. Why doesn't he say something? I wondered. 'Hang on a minute!' I was about to shout, when I suddenly realised that the blanket was still humped over a bulky form. Somehow, the man was on the stretcher at the same time as standing beside the chair.

Confused, I watched the ambulancemen continue through the crowd with their burden, followed by the man who was looking slightly puzzled but not in any pain at all.

What am I seeing? I asked myself. Is this an hallucination? But deep down I knew the answer already. It was just as Danny Lester had told me – I was seeing a spirit, the way I always had done, only this time I was seeing it seconds after it had been released from its old body.

The baffling thing was, why was *I* being shown such a thing when, from what I could make out, nobody else in that crowd had been granted such a view? This was a question I couldn't answer. Life was getting more complicated by the second and I didn't know what to make of it. I just wanted to be a normal teenager like my friends, I told myself. Perhaps if I ignored the weird part of myself – the part Mum had always either dismissed as attention-seeking or urged me to keep secret for fear of being thought peculiar – it would just go away of its own accord.

I went home to find another note through the door from the nurse. My father was even more poorly, it seemed, and wanted to know why I hadn't been back to see him. He was asking for me again.

'You'd better go,' Mum said. 'He might be at death's door.'

This time my brother came as well. Horrible as our father had been to him, he still had feelings for the man and perhaps he hoped that poor health might have softened him and made him into the dad we would all have liked him to be.

But if that's what my brother had been secretly hoping, he was in for a disappointment. We found our father in a filthy temper, being rude to the nurses and raging at the world.

The gangrene had spread and he'd had to have his leg amputated. He was sitting in bed, more drawn and sallow than before, with a rigid cage under the covers keeping the sheets off his bad leg. A sickening smell of dried blood hung in the air and he was obviously in pain.

'Why me?' he was complaining. 'I'm going to lose everything now. I don't think I'll be able to walk again. My life's ruined! Why did it have to happen to me?'

Normally I'm the most soft-hearted of people, but for once I couldn't dredge up any sympathy. Why *not* you? I found myself saying silently. You've been a terrible person and, boy, hasn't it come back on you now? It made me think of a slogan I'd seen recently on a T-shirt: 'What goes around, comes around.' I wouldn't wish suffering on anyone, but it was certainly true in my father's case.

The visit was not a success. My father hardly acknowledged my brother and didn't ask after Debbie. All he wanted to do was moan about the unfairness of his lot and shout at the nurses.

I left as soon as I could and I made up my mind that I wouldn't go back, no matter how many scribbled notes came through the door.

I never saw my father again. Not alive anyway.

Chapter Eight

Maybe it was because I missed Gladys, or maybe it was my lifelong desire to have a granny, but when Mum moved on from the café to work in an old people's home I couldn't keep away from the place. I popped in so often to 'help' Mum that I ended up becoming a voluntary worker.

There were a great many brass pipes in the old building that the strict matron insisted must be kept gleaming, so one of my jobs was to polish them up till they shone. There was another young girl, Paula, helping alongside me and she was given the task of cleaning the old people's false teeth. I helped her collect them in their boxes from each of the nine bedrooms and then we took them to the scullery for cleaning.

While I was hunting for another tin of Brasso for my pipes, Paula decided to streamline her denture cleaning procedure. She found a big bowl in the cupboard, filled it with water and sterilising solution and then tipped in all the false teeth. Round and round they went in the bowl and they came up a treat. There was only one small problem: when she laid them out on the draining board afterwards they all looked exactly the same.

'Oh!' I heard Paula gasp behind me. 'Oh dear.'

I turned to see nine sets of sparkling gnashers grinning up at us from the sink and a bewildered looking Paula staring at them helplessly.

'I don't know whose is whose,' she said. 'I can't give them the wrong teeth. They won't fit will they? Oh dear.'

I burst out laughing and the teeth giggled noiselessly back at me from the draining board.

'Don't worry,' I told Paula, 'I think I can guess.'

'How can you? They all look the same.'

'I just can, that's all,' I said. 'I'm a good guesser.'

I had made up my mind to be a normal teenager and not use my weird ways, but this was different. No-one would know and I didn't want Paula to get into trouble.

I picked up one of the boxes and it gave a tiny little tug against my fingers towards a set of dentures at the back of the pile.

'I reckon these are the ones,' I said, putting the teeth into the box and picking up another one, 'and these . . .' I fished out another set, 'go in here.'

'How can you possibly tell?' said Paula.

'Well, we'll soon see when we give them back, won't we?'

Paula looked even more worried then, but there was no alternative. We took the boxes back to the rooms without a word and the next day, to her astonishment, nothing was said. No-one complained, so we could only assume that my guesses had been right. Either that or the old people were so accustomed to poorly-fitting teeth that they didn't notice the difference.

One of my favourite old ladies was a wonderful little woman called Anna who said she was 113 and swore by a spoonful of honey in her porridge every morning. Everyone thought she was senile, but she sounded sensible enough to me and I loved to listen to her talking about the Victorian days and the old-fashioned way they did things then.

Another wonderful character was Violet, who must have been well over 90 herself, though she certainly couldn't attribute her long life to healthy living.

'I used to be a prostitute you know,' she said, and a passing nurse raised her eyebrows and shook her head at such wild fantasises. But I had a sudden picture of a pretty young Violet laughing provocatively and tossing a scarlet feather boa round her neck, so I believed her totally.

Violet liked me to paint her fingernails for her, and her toenails too if I had time. And sometimes I'd find her holding a mirror up in her shaky hands and trying to put red lipstick on.

'I'm just off out on the pull dear,' she'd say, hobbling towards the door with her Zimmer frame. 'I need a punter.'

And I'd gently turn her round and guide her back.

'Oh not tonight Violet. It's pouring out there. There's no-one about. It's not worth it.'

Violet had beautifully soft skin, a halo of white hair and a really angelic face, yet she'd had such a rough life.

She was put up for prostitution when she was 13, she told me, and there was no alternative.

One day I saw all these children clustered around her, but they vanished when I approached and later Violet told me that years back she'd learned how to give herself DIY abortions. A gruesome tale involving a bucket, some water and a length of hosepipe.

The other residents were just as interesting as Violet in their own way and I loved my work. I enjoyed it so much that I gave up being a kitchen assistant at Peter Jones and started temping for social services.

One night as I was going home I saw an old lady, one of our residents, coming along the corridor towards me.

'Hello Diane!' she said, smiling.

'Hello Mary,' I replied, but then without warning the Lined Man was beside me.

'Watch,' he said.

And as I watched I saw a man arrive at Mary's side. He was very smart in a tweed suit with a paisley scarf round his neck. He smiled at Mary in a fond way and although she didn't seem to be aware of him, he accompanied her down the corridor and the pair of them disappeared round the corner. It seemed clear to me that he was her husband.

'What . . . ?' I asked the Lined Man.

'Ssshhhh,' he said. 'Look at Mary. Think about this and learn.'

And then he was gone.

I sighed. Sometimes the Lined Man really annoyed me. Either he didn't answer my questions or he gave me answers which only led to more questions. He wouldn't even tell me his name, though I often asked who he was. 'Wait and see. All will be revealed when it's time. You're here to learn. You must find the answers for yourself.'

I shrugged my shoulders. Well, there wasn't time to puzzle over it now, I had a bus to catch.

The next day when I arrived at the care home there was a lot of bustling about going on and I saw the doctor's car driving away.

'Is something wrong?' I asked, as I pushed open the swing door.

'Mary passed away in the night,' said one of the staff. 'We've got to get her room sorted.'

And something clicked in my mind. That was what the Lined Man wanted to show me: Mary's husband had come for her when it was her time to leave. I realised that the link of love is never broken – even after a person passes on.

After that I noticed that I frequently saw the spirits of loved ones coming close to residents who were to pass away shortly afterwards. It was disturbing to know in advance what was going to happen, but oddly comforting too. It was nice to think that those elderly men and women were going to be reunited with people who still so obviously cared for them.

As I became more experienced I got sent to a wider variety of care homes, some of which were for people who were sick. One morning at a nursing home I went to take a meal in to an elderly man called Jack. Jack was sitting in a chair by the window. He was pale and thin but his eyes glittered with spirit.

'Don't think I can manage much today, love,' he said as I put the tray down. 'I've got a bit of a pain.'

'I'm sorry to hear that,' I said. 'Where's your pain then?'

Jack patted his stomach, over the bowel area. 'All round here,' he said and as I looked, my eyes seemed to go right through his protecting hand and I was seeing an ugly mass of black inside. It was cancer, I knew instantly.

Oh my God! I thought. But I forced myself to smile.

'I know, Jack. Why don't I go and see if I can get you something for the pain?'

From then on I could tell which of the patients had cancer and which ones were about to pass away. As a care assistant, though, it wasn't my place to start diagnosing people; no-one would have listened to me even if I had, and I could see that there was no point anyway because it was time for these elderly people to go. What's more, I was very hesitant about saying any-thing that might draw attention to my unusual talent. I didn't want jewellery and people's hands thrust in front of me again.

We also had a lot of multiple sclerosis sufferers and these made me particularly sad because they were such young people. There was a pretty woman called Glenys with attractive olive skin and well-cut clothes, but she was in a wheelchair and when she tried to talk her head kept jerking. We had to hold her head for her so that she could have a conversation. She liked to tell me about her lovely family: her beautiful, intelligent children and her husband.

'Of course he's got another lady now, my husband,' said Glenys, 'but I don't mind, because look at me! Who can blame him?'

And I used to cry all the way home, thinking about how she'd lost everything just because she'd fallen ill.

I often shed tears over the MS sufferers. Some of them died so young I would come off duty really upset. It was very difficult to deal with. I didn't mind how hard I worked to try to make these poor people more comfortable, but there weren't enough staff to go round and the buzzers from the patients' rooms would be going all day long. Sometimes I'd run down the corridor for the umpteenth time in response to the latest emergency and I'd be so tired I'd be thinking, 'I hope someone else gets there first.' But nine times out of ten it was just me.

In the end I overdid it so much I got a very bad case of tennis elbow. My arm locked completely in one position and refused to budge. I had to take time off and have a series of cortisone injections to free it up.

I was so busy I rarely had time to think, but every now and then there was a pause and it occurred to me that, even though I was trying to ignore the strange side of my mind, the more I experienced of the world, the more weirdness I discovered in myself.

'You know what,' I said to my cousin Julie one night when I was enjoying a rare evening off. 'Why don't we go back to Danny Lester and see what he makes of us now?'

'Good idea,' said Julie. 'I've heard he moved but I'll see if I can find out where he's gone.'

It didn't take her long. Danny had moved nearer to the coast and now occupied a terraced house overlooking the sea at the Mumbles. Julie and I made an appointment for a Saturday and we arrived to find about eight people in front of us, all arranged on dining room chairs round the waiting room. It felt like being at the doctor's.

Julie nudged me. 'Still got the same jug and bowl sets I see!' she whispered, and sure enough, on every available surface the identical pieces of china were laid out.

His friendly wife ushered me upstairs when my turn finally came and this time I wasn't as frightened as I'd been before. I knew what to expect. Yet there'd been a change in Danny. He'd lost his spark. He ushered me to a chair and regarded me solemnly. He looked old and tired, there were big dark shadows under his eyes and he slouched back against the table, half sitting, half standing, as if he was too weary to hold himself upright. Something appeared to be troubling him. It seemed to me that he was spending too much time with the dead and not enough with his feet on the ground talking to that nice wife of his.

'You've got something on your mind,' said Danny, fixing me with a piercing eye. 'Come on, say it lovely girl. Don't hide it.'

He didn't seem to remember me from the previous

visit, which was not surprising as it had been several years before, but I was still a little nervous.

'I was just thinking you seem a bit tired,' I ventured tactfully, 'I think maybe you're working too hard.'

Danny gave a wry laugh. 'You're probably right, lovely girl. You're probably right. But you know what? One of these days you'll know exactly how tired I feel because you'll be doing it too. You're going to be known world-wide for your gift. In fact – you're going to be the next Doris Stokes!'

I was stunned. Doris Stokes was the top medium of the day, a household name who had appeared at the London Palladium and filled the Sydney Opera House three times. How on earth could Danny possibly think that an ordinary girl from Swansea like me, with no GCSEs, could possibly do anything like that? 'You're strange!' I thought to myself.

Then Danny seemed to come back down to earth a bit. 'You don't seem to realise it – you think you haven't got a grandmother, but she's always with you too,' he said. 'In fact she saved you the other night. You nearly fell down the stairs and she caught you.'

I was amazed. Just the week before, I'd gone out with my friends to a pub with live music upstairs. After-wards, as we were picking our way down the steep staircase in our high boots, laughing and chatting, I caught one of my heels in the turn-up of my trousers and pitched forwards. I really thought I was going to fall headfirst down the steps but then, just as my body began to go, I was jerked back, almost as if some unseen hand had pulled me, and the next second I was upright and grabbing the banister rail. It was pretty scary at the time, and looking back I suddenly realised that Danny must be right.

And when I mentioned it to Mum later that day I discovered that the incident was even more spooky than I'd thought. Mum reminded me that her mother had passed over as the result of an accident in which *she* fell down the stairs of a Swansea pub – the very same pub which was now a magnet for young people with its music nights. Gran obviously didn't want history repeating itself.

Danny went on to tell me a number of other small details about my life, family members and a forthcoming holiday and then he said: 'And you'll be getting married soon. But you won't stay with him.'

My mouth dropped open. I wasn't wearing my ring, but unknown to Danny I'd just agreed to get engaged.

Chapter Nine

It all happened because I missed my bus. I hadn't intended to be late home that night but I was 18, I'd been out with friends for the evening, we'd got chatting and I'd ended up staying longer than I planned. Walking down the road with one of the girls afterwards we both saw my bus disappearing round the corner. There was absolutely no point in running.

'Oh no!' I muttered.

'Never mind Di,' said Susie, 'I'm meeting some friends in the pub just down from here. Why don't you come in and phone for a taxi? You can talk to us while you wait.'

'Okay,' I said. It was a cold night, there weren't many buses home to Don and Mum's and I didn't fancy walking. So I followed Susie into the cosy bar and of course it was quite a while before I got round to finding the phone.

Somehow I found myself chatting to a nice young man (I'll call him Gwyn) with a vaguely different accent. He was from North Wales where, to us South Wales types, the voices sound deeper and more exotic. He was very smart and neat with dark hair and the most beautiful white teeth. He had excellent manners, beautifully manicured hands and a lovely smile that lit up his eyes and his whole face.

Funnily enough when he smiled, instead of thinking how good-looking he was – which he was – I found myself reflecting, 'A man with a smile as lovely as that is never going to hurt me.' It didn't strike me as an odd reaction at the time, but obviously without even knowing it, growing up with my father had left me with a certain wariness about men.

We talked and talked and Gwyn impressed me more by the second. He was in the Royal Navy and whether it was his naval training I don't know, but he seemed so much more polite than the boys I normally met. He was older than me, eight years older as it turned out, but he appeared to be the perfect gentleman. I ended up staying two hours and then Gwyn offered me a lift home, but I said no. I stuck to my plan of getting a taxi.

Although I'd enjoyed the evening, I wasn't that bothered about seeing Gwyn again, but he began phoning me and before I knew it we were dating. Gwyn became my first proper boyfriend. He was away a lot with his ship, but when he came home he took me out and he always treated me well. Being in his mid twenties he seemed more mature and sensible than the local boys. He didn't drink and he was quite particular about keeping fit. He ran marathons, drank good-quality orange juice and always looked well pressed and scrupulously clean. I liked a man who took a pride in his appearance and, although I wasn't madly in love with him, I enjoyed our dates.

Debbie by this time had married and left home. She hadn't intended to get married so soon (she was only 18) but she'd met her S. R. – Stephen Radford – as predicted years before, and he was a soldier in the Welsh Guards about to be sent to the Falkland Islands. So they had decided to bring the wedding forward in case anything happened.

It was a whirlwind ceremony, Debbie was a very pretty bride and now that the war was over she'd gone to live in married quarters with Stephen. I missed her terribly, but her absence meant that her bedroom at Don's was free.

'Why don't I lodge in Debbie's old room when I'm home on leave?' Gwyn suggested one day. And it seemed the ideal solution. There was no point in renting a flat that would be empty for weeks at a time while he was at sea.

Yet although everyone agreed with the arrangement, it seemed to bring out an unexpectedly old-fashioned streak in Don.

'You ought to be engaged,' he grumbled. 'Living under the same roof – people'll get the wrong idea. Are you going to get engaged?'

Gwyn seemed to think this was an excellent suggestion.

'Well, why don't we get engaged then?' he asked me. 'Would you like to?'

I hesitated. It seemed the right thing to do and I was very fond of Gwyn. He would make a good husband. And yet something held me back. The Lined Man moved in to speak softly in my ear, but by now I'd learned that if I ignored him very firmly he'd go. So I closed my ears and pushed him away. I didn't want advice. I was an adult and I wanted to make my own decisions without help. The Lined Man took the hint and faded away. Clearly he realised I needed to make my own mistakes.

Debbie was married with a baby on the way now, and a lot of my friends were getting engaged. Gwyn, at 27, was the perfect age for a man to settle down and I was old enough myself. There seemed no reason to say no.

'I'd love to,' I told Gwyn.

And when he presented me with a beautiful diamond solitaire ring a few days later, I was thrilled.

I felt very grown up as I walked around flashing my engagement ring and admiring it sparkling away on my finger. I'm a proper engaged woman, I told myself proudly. And yet there were times when I looked at it and I got the strangest feeling that it was slightly second-hand.

I also heard whispers: 'It won't last', 'It's not right', and when Danny Lester seemed to confirm that we wouldn't stay together I began to get quite alarmed. Yet Gwyn had done nothing wrong. How could I break his heart over such insubstantial fears and imaginings?

I pushed all the doubts to the back of my mind and refused to think about them, which was surprisingly easy, especially with Gwyn being away so much.

The months went on. I began to crave a little home of my own that I could decorate as I pleased and my auntie, who rented out the cottage next door to her house said that I could take it over. I put up gingham curtains and filled the place with flowers, pretty table-cloths and cushions, and when he was home Gwyn stayed with me instead of Don.

After a while Gwyn tired of the sea and took a job as an ambulanceman. This meant a spell of retraining but eventually he would be able to settle down to proper married life. He started looking out for family homes, because we knew we both wanted children once we were married, and in 1986 he said he'd found the perfect place. It was a bright, modern, mid-terraced house, surprisingly spacious inside and situated on a smart estate.

I loved it.

'We'd better arrange the wedding then,' said Gwyn.

The voices in my mind came crowding back but I shoved them ruthlessly out of the way. I was twenty years old now, I reminded myself, quite grown-up enough to know my own mind. I'd agreed to marry Gwyn, I wore his engagement ring and I'd keep my promise. And closing my ears to the Lined Man and all the other doubters, I set off in search of the perfect wedding dress.

The ceremony was fixed for June 13 – the only summer Saturday still available, probably because of the date, but it didn't bother us. We weren't superstitious, we told each other. Why should we be scared of a number?

Mum had recently completed a professional cookery

course and was keen to show off her enhanced skills, so she offered to do the catering. Debbie arranged to come over from Germany with her little daughter Louise, now 2, who was to be a flower girl, and I found myself a wonderful dress in the window of a bridal shop. It was a romantic, off-the-shoulder affair with a big *Gone-With-The-Wind* skirt and nipped-in waist and I planned to team it with a hat, parasol and bouquet of peach and cream roses. To top it all, we hired a vintage Rolls-Royce to take me to the church and a talented photographer to create dreamy pictures at Clare Park, a nearby beauty spot. What bride could ask for a happier occasion?

Yet I couldn't quite muster the excitement I'd expected to feel. If I'm honest I was probably happier to meet up with Debbie again when she arrived from Germany than I was contemplating my wedding.

I was staying at Don's house for the night before the big day and Mum gave Debbie and me a celebratory bottle of Martini with which to enjoy my hen night. We sat up half the night chatting, sipping our drinks and admiring the wedding finery.

At some point the phone rang. It was Gwyn.

'I'm allergic to something!' he told me in anguish. 'My face has swollen up. I look terrible! The doctor doesn't know what it is but I look like the Elephant Man. Do you still want to marry me looking like this?'

I was stunned. What a dreadful thing to happen! Gwyn had never been allergic to anything before. My mind flitted to the romantic pictures on the little white bridge in Clyne Park. They wouldn't look so romantic with an elephant-man groom. But how could I say that to Gwyn? He felt bad enough as it was.

'Of course I still want to marry you,' I said kindly, 'and anyway, I'm sure you'll feel a lot better by tomorrow. It'll probably have gone down by then.'

But I felt a little tremble of fear. Was this the curse of the thirteenth? Or was the Lined Man trying to move my bridegroom out of the way just as the bully Jackie was removed from the scene all those years ago on the day she intended to beat me up? Well, whatever it was, it wasn't going to work.

The next morning I went through the motions, taking a long bath, getting my hair done, helping Debbie dress Louise – who looked a picture. Eventually everything was finished and there I was, a Welsh Scarlett O'Hara in my *Gone-With-The-Wind* dress, peach-trimmed parasol in my hand. The weather was beautiful. The sun shone from a cloudless blue sky and the silver Mercedes, decked out with white ribbons, pulled up in the street. Curious neighbours began coming to their gates to watch and Don, who was to give me away, led me to the door.

Yet there must have been something in the air that day.

'D'you want to change your mind, Diane?' he asked suddenly. 'You don't have to get into the car. Nobody will think any the less of you.'

'Yes, Diane,' said Mum, pausing as she hurried by, hat askew, 'it's not too late. You don't have to go through with it.'

I thought of all the beautiful salmon en croutes and the other exquisite food Mum had spent four days lovingly preparing; I thought of poor Gwyn waiting at the church. How could I do that to him, or to Mum?

Yet still I hesitated. Shall I or shan't I, I thought, hovering on the step. I was so tempted to turn back. But I didn't. I didn't have the guts.

'No, I'm fine,' I assured Don. 'Let's go.'

'Well, as long as you're certain,' he said doubtfully. And adjusting the peach carnation in his buttonhole he led me down the path and into the car.

Despite everything I'd said to Gwyn, I was shocked when I saw him at the altar. His face was still swollen, his eyes were puffy slits and he was covered in red blotches. The poor man should not have tried to get married that day, but what else could he do? He didn't want to let me down any more than I wanted to let him down.

So we went through with it. We posed for the romantic pictures and we ate Mum's delicious spread, and afterwards, instead of a honeymoon, we went back to our new house and spent a few days shopping for furniture.

Life went on much as before. Gwyn was away a lot on courses and I was working hard in social services. One day I popped along to the doctor for advice about starting a family. I'd been suffering from endometriosis and I'd heard that this condition could make conception difficult.

'Well, it'll probably take you a bit longer than most,' said the doctor, 'so allow yourself plenty of time.'

Talk about famous last words. I assumed he meant a couple of years, but I got pregnant almost immediately. My career was going well and it was a bit sooner than I expected, but I was thrilled. I couldn't wait to have a baby of my own. Gwyn was pleased too and yet, something odd was happening between us – or maybe it was just to me.

It was years now since I'd seen my father. The last I heard of him he'd been discharged from hospital and had spun grumpily away in a wheelchair, still railing bitterly about his misfortune and showing every sign of taking to drink in a big way. I was very glad I'd resolved never to see him again. He was the last person I wanted in my life right now. Yet as the pregnancy went on, I found my mind going back to him again and again and I'd hear his voice.

Gwyn only had to ask me what there was to eat and my father's furious roar would echo down the years: 'Where's my dinner, woman?'

One evening I came home tired from work and went to sit down.

'That's my chair,' Gwyn said, moving towards it.

Instantly there was a flash in my mind and I was six years old again, watching in confusion as my father yanked away the seat just as Mum was about to sit down so that she crashed to the floor. I froze.

'Well, I do usually sit there,' said Gwyn.

I backed away from him.

'Have it then,' I said, and that's when I knew for certain that I wasn't going to be with him for long.

Lisa was born on November 22 1987, an exquisite little thing with big dark blue eyes and beautiful cherry-red lips. I was on a cloud of happiness. I couldn't stop cuddling my lovely little girl. But after a while the nurses came to take her away.

'You need some sleep,' they said to me in their well-meaning way.

But I felt bereft. I didn't want to part with her and I hadn't realised they take the babies away soon after birth so that the mums can rest. I didn't want to rest. I wanted to sit with Lisa, so once the nurses had gone I slipped down to the room where they'd taken her for the night, and cuddled her till morning. I was on such a high there was no way I could sleep.

I loved being a mum and Gwyn was a proud dad, though his job still kept him away from home on residential courses quite a lot. Money was a bit tight, so when Lisa started toddling Mum suggested I went back to work part-time while she looked after her. I thoroughly enjoyed being a full-time mum but my wages were badly needed and the system worked well. Mum adored Lisa and spoiled her rotten and it was nice for me to keep one toe in the grown-up world of work.

Everything was going well and I was looking forward to our first Christmas together as a proper little family. I'd bought masses of presents as usual and Mum, who was getting more professional with her cooking by the minute, had offered to bone my turkey for me. So on Christmas Eve I wrapped up the bird and was just about to hurry out of the door to put it in the car, when the mirror on the wall caught my eye. It didn't look right. And with a sinking heart I saw that it had misted over as if it was full of cloud.

A horrible fear gripped my stomach. Something awful was going to happen.

I drove over to Mum as if I was driving on ice and when I walked in she looked at my worried face in concern.

'What's the matter with you?' she asked.

'Something awful is going to happen,' I said. 'This is going to be the worst Christmas ever.'

Mum was probably unnerved by this but she struggled to be positive. 'Don't talk nonsense, Diane. This is going to be a lovely Christmas. Everyone's fine and I'm going to make you a beautiful turkey, so stop fussing. Why don't you have a glass of wine?'

I shook my head. I never have even so much as a mouthful of alcohol if I'm driving. Mum did her best to reassure me, then I unpacked the turkey and went on my way to work through the lists of tasks still to be completed before Christmas Day.

I had to drive through a busy part of Swansea and, still taking the utmost care, I turned off the main road into a narrow side street. Just as I rounded the corner a little girl with bright red hair walking along with her mum caught my eye. The next second the girl ran straight out into the road in front of me. I slammed on the brakes in an emergency stop and the terrified mother pulled the child to safety.

'Thank you!' she mouthed at me, hugging the little girl tightly to her before telling her off.

I smiled to show it was okay. I understood. And relief flowed through me. That must have been the incident the mirror was warning me about. Fortunately I'd been on my guard and averted a nasty accident. I waved to the two figures on the pavement as I moved slowly off again. Ahead of me on my right was a big warehouse with Christmas trees outside filling the pavement. A delivery van was pulled up at the kerb, either loading or unloading them, and on my left an old man with a carrier bag was walking unsteadily down the road.

Just as my eyes rested on him he suddenly swung off the pavement and lurched out in front of me. I screeched the brakes again and tried to swerve out of his way, but the delivery van was in my path and I couldn't go far. The corner of my bumper just caught him and he fell to the ground.

Horrified, I jumped out of the car. At least he couldn't be badly hurt, I thought, because I was going so slowly. I'd only just moved off after stopping to avoid the red-haired girl. But when I looked at the pathetic figure on the ground I felt faint. His leg was broken and the bone was sticking right through his trouser leg.

'Help me! Help me!' he was crying weakly.

His bag had fallen beside him and a smashed whisky bottle was pouring amber liquid all over the tarmac.

Fighting down the urge to be sick, I tore off my coat

and covered him with it. Someone had called an ambulance and they were there in seconds, followed by the police. 'I was going so slowly. How could he be so badly hurt?' I kept asking the ambulancemen.

'It's his age, such brittle bones,' said the man, tucking a thick blanket round the frail casualty, 'and he must have fallen awkwardly.'

The policeman came over to me and caught the pungent whiff of whisky fumes hanging in the air. 'Have you been drinking, madam?'

'No,' I said, but they breathalysed me anyway. Thank goodness I hadn't accepted that glass of wine from Mum.

The old man was taken away to hospital and I realised I knew him. He was one of the residents at the old people's home where I worked. He was over ninety and quite blind. He shouldn't have been out on his own but he was an independent old fellow. He'd lived in the area all his life so he thought he knew the streets like the back of his hand. He'd slipped away when no-one was looking to treat himself to a bit of Christmas cheer.

When I went to visit him later he was very nice about it. 'Wasn't your fault, love,' he said. 'You couldn't help it. I just walked out.'

But I was devastated. Throughout the Christmas holiday I kept replaying the horrific scene in my mind, and to make matters worse the man's relatives made it known that they were going to sue me. Fortunately, a witness came forward to testify that the accident was not my fault and a few weeks later the matter was dropped, but the stress and worry over the festive season made it without doubt my worst Christmas so far. Once again my mysterious mirror had told me the truth. I just wished it could be a bit more specific over the details.

Day-to-day life continued as normal and on the surface we must have appeared to be the ideal modern family with our good jobs, perfect child and lovely home. Yet underneath, undetected by anyone else, the malevolent influence of my father hung about the house. The past refused to stay buried; it flickered before my eyes when I least expected it.

One day I was putting on my make-up, ready to go to work, when the mirror went misty again. Without thinking I wiped it with my fingers, but the haziness didn't clear. It's not an omen, I told myself, I've gone too heavy-handed with the bathroom cleaner and left bad smears. Yet the mirror refused all attempts to polish it clean. I stared at it in dismay. Something bad's going to happen.

I turned away quickly. No it's not! I told myself firmly and went downstairs. Yet all day I felt apprehensive. Work was uneventful and I came home to find Gwyn watching sport on TV and Lisa sitting on the stairs. All was peaceful. Everything was fine and it was the end of the day. The mirror had been wrong, I said to myself, breathing a sigh of relief. It was nothing more than a smeary glass after all. I would stop being so fanciful and next time I'd try that old-fashioned cleaning tip with vinegar and newspaper.

I went into the kitchen to start dinner and Lisa asked

if she could put a kids' video on. Unfortunately Gwyn
was still watching his match and he was reluctant to
turn it off at a crucial point in the game. A stupid
argument sprang up. We had disagreements like any
couple but they were usually soon over, yet for some
reason this one kept on throughout the evening.

In the end I got so cross that at bedtime I went into
Lisa's room and climbed into the top bunk. I lay there
for a while but I couldn't get comfortable. The little
children's pillow was too thin for me so I slipped down
the ladder to fetch my own from the big double bed I
normally shared with Gwyn.

Gwyn was already tucked in under the duvet when I
crept into the room. He was either asleep or in a huff
ignoring me, so I reached out stealthily for my pillow.
But just as my fingers closed on the cotton pillowcase a
heavy arm suddenly swung out from the bed and
caught me a tremendous blow across the face and head.
I yelled and jumped back and Gwyn sat up all confused
and apologetic. He'd been asleep, he kept saying, he was
startled, he didn't realise I was there.

My ear was clanging like Big Ben and when I put my
fingers up to it I felt blood on my hand.

'I'm sorry, Diane. I didn't mean it,' Gwyn was saying,
but my stomach knotted up and I ran out of the room
in sudden terror.

I was back in the lounge of Mum and Dad's big house.
It was Saturday afternoon, Dad was stretched out
snoring on the green settee and Mum was trying to
wake him. As her nervous fingers touched his shoulder,

his arm lashed out, quick as a cobra and hit her a hefty blow.

I couldn't get the image out of my mind. I ran into the bathroom and locked the door. No matter how Gwyn knocked and hammered, no matter how he pleaded and insisted he was sorry and that it was an accident – I wouldn't come out. Nothing would wipe away those memories.

The next morning, after he'd gone to work, I phoned Debbie, herself now divorced from Stephen and back in Swansea.

'Call a London cab, put Lisa and all your stuff in it and come straight round,' she said.

Which is exactly what I did. And as I scrabbled in the bathroom cupboard for my shampoo and face creams I couldn't help noticing that the mirror was now bright and sparkling. Which was more than I was. My eyes were red from crying, my eardrum was perforated and my marriage was over.

Chapter Ten

It was nearly Christmas and Debbie and I, single mums that we both now were – to my secret shame as I hated the idea of being a divorced mother – were determined to give the children the best Christmas ever.

Lisa and I had moved out of Debbie's little house and were staying in a small but very comfortable apartment nearby, which was also convenient for Mum and Don's. The arrangement worked well because Mum, who loved her grandchildren, could baby-sit for us both and it freed Debbie and I to enjoy a few nights out together and to stage peaceful shopping trips without having to worry about the little ones.

As Christmas approached Debbie and I had hit the stores – spending far more than we could really afford on presents for the children but we were desperate to make up for the fact that their dads wouldn't be there. (Gwyn had moved away and Stephen was abroad.) We didn't want them to miss out.

I had a stack of things to wrap which were hidden in the back of my wardrobe, so one night after Lisa was in bed I surrounded myself with scissors, Sellotape and enough snowman and Santa paper to decorate the whole flat, and cut and stuck and trimmed until I was so tired I could hardly keep my eyes open.

I just had time to shove armfuls of crackly red and white parcels back in the wardrobe before I fell onto the bed, fast asleep.

I was exhausted, yet I had the oddest dream. I was asleep I was sure, yet I was dreaming I was wide awake. I was sitting up in bed and there, standing by my feet, was my cousin Peter.

The last time I'd seen Peter, who was now a corporal in the army and stationed in Germany with his family, had been months ago when he was home on leave visiting his mum in Swansea. He'd given me a big hug and swung Lisa around till she squealed with delight and was generally his old lovely self. However, he didn't think he'd be able to get home for Christmas and Auntie Kathleen was resigned to the fact that she'd have to wait until after the festive season to see him.

Yet now it seemed he'd been able to get away after all. He was dressed in his ordinary clothes, blue shirt and jeans – not army uniform – and his fair hair gleamed as if sunshine was pouring on it. The only odd thing was that my bedroom was lit up brighter than I'd ever seen it before by a dazzling light from behind Peter's shoulder.

'Peter!' I said in delight. 'How . . . ?'

He looked at me with an odd expression for a second and then he gave me his big, slow, reassuring smile.

'But . . . did you . . . ?' I began. 'I mean, have you . . . ?'

Peter just smiled and then somehow he wasn't there

any more. There was an empty space where he'd been standing. The light faded and my room went dull. In my dream this didn't seem strange; I just lay down again, pulled the covers back over me and returned to sleep.

Hours later, when I woke up properly, the oddness of the dream began to sink in. How peculiar, I said to myself. I haven't thought of Peter for ages and suddenly I'm dreaming about him and not even a proper dream at that. But then the phone was ringing and Lisa woke up, so I dragged on my dressing gown and rushed out to answer it.

It was Mum.

'Diane, I've got terrible news,' she said, and she sounded as if she'd been crying, 'It's Peter . . .'

My stomach turned over. 'My God I was just dreaming about Peter,' I said.

'He's dead. There's been some sort of accident, I'm not sure what happened. Auntie Kath's in a terrible state.'

Peter was Mum's favourite. He was the favourite of all of us because he was such a kind, thoughtful person. Gradually the dreadful story emerged. The previous night Peter, who was brilliant at crafts and creative hobbies, had been making decorations for the splendid Christmas tree he intended to put up for his two children. He'd taken a break and popped out for a quick drink with a friend, then he'd come back to resume the decorations late into the night while the children were asleep.

At some point he went to the bathroom, taking the

newspaper with him to read. No-one knows exactly what happened next; we can only assume he fell asleep because he slipped off the loo and cracked his head on the floor. He was found dead the next morning, the newspaper spread on the tiles beneath him. He was only 33 years old.

I was devastated. Why hadn't I realised? Why hadn't I seen the significance of that dream? And then I was filled with anger. Why did it have to be Peter? Why do they always take the best?

My wicked father was probably still going strong, still busily making people's lives a misery while Peter, who only ever tried to help anyone, was dead. My mind went back to all the times my tall, handsome cousin had looked after me; all the ice-creams he'd bought me with his own pocket money; all the magnificent sandcastles he'd built and let me jump on . . .

'What did he say?' Mum was asking.

'What?'

'What did he say when you saw him in the night?' She was finally getting used to my funny ways and was beginning to believe they might mean something. 'Did he explain . . . Did he say what happened?'

'He didn't say anything,' I snuffled, wiping away my tears with the sleeve of my dressing gown. 'He was just standing there smiling. He looked fine . . .'

'He didn't seem shocked. Or in pain?'

'No. If anything he looked happy . . .'

Mum sighed. 'Tell Kath. Maybe it'll help.'

I sobbed and sobbed when I put the phone down and

poor little Lisa couldn't understand what was wrong. Yet even through my tears I puzzled over that dream. It nagged away at me. What did it mean? Peter had looked so real, so solid. Could he really have been there in my room that night? Could he have stepped out of his body just as I'd seen the man in Peter Jones do years ago, and come to me? Was it not really a dream at all?

That night as I lay in bed I whispered to the Lined Man, 'Are you there? What happened last night?', and then I added angrily, 'And why take Peter? Why him? We need him here.'

There was a silence for a while, then the Lined Man said in his inscrutable way, 'Trust and learn. Just trust.'

But I was in no mood for that sort of advice. If there really was a spirit world out there, it had let me down very badly.

Not long afterwards Peter's body was flown back to Wales and so many people wanted to come to the funeral that the church was overflowing. It was a very sad day. Auntie Kathleen was distraught, so was Peter's wife Joanne, and everyone else dabbed at their red-rimmed eyes and blew their noses constantly.

Yet as I walked with a heavy heart up the path towards the church, I stopped dead and almost did a double take. There was Peter. Not in a coffin but standing outside, a little apart from the other mourners and looking very much as he'd looked the last time he'd dropped in to say hello to Mum. He wasn't trailing ghostly white sheets; he glowed with health. He was dressed in blue trousers and a light shirt and there was a serious, slightly puzzled expression on his face as his friends and relatives filed past just inches from his shoes without appearing to see him. Then he glanced up, noticed me, our eyes met and he smiled.

This was all so peculiar I wanted to pinch myself. It was one thing to be asleep in bed and dreaming of seeing him, but to be wide awake and glimpse him gathered with the rest of the congregation at his own funeral was bizarre verging on madness.

I'd never even been to a funeral before, let alone the funeral of a young person, and although in the past I'd witnessed spirits walking away from their own recently-deceased corpses, it had just never occurred to me that they might turn up to watch their own funerals.

Peter was dead, I told myself sternly. Everyone was crying and this couldn't be happening. In a way I wanted to see him because I didn't want him to be dead, but if he really was dead it was very unsettling to see him walking about. Perhaps I really was going crazy? You hear of people going insane with grief, perhaps that had happened to me. I turned away and told myself firmly that the vision of Peter was all in my mind. Yet as I passed briskly through the church door I couldn't help seeing the glint of his fair head out of the corner of my eye . . .

The next few weeks were a confusing time. I minded Peter's beloved son and daughter while Joanne dealt with the endless list of things that need sorting when something like this happens. But everything I picked up, every toy the children showed me, tingled with the presence of their father. I knew which items he'd given them, which had belonged to Peter and where he'd kept them. Yet I didn't feel I could say anything to the children in case I upset them.

Christmas wasn't much fun that year and Mum was worried about Auntie Kathleen who was taking it very badly.

'Would you give her a ring, Diane?' asked Mum on her return from a visit. 'If you can get anything about Peter it might help.'

Auntie Kathleen had always been a bit sceptical about such things but Mum had confided in her in the past about my strange ways and now she was so grief-stricken she was ready to clutch at any straws that might cheer her up. I'd be glad to try. I dialled her number with slow fingers. This wouldn't be easy, I knew, yet as soon as I heard her dull voice on the other end of the line, it was as if Peter had jumped into the hall with me. I couldn't see him but I could feel him almost at my shoulder.

'Hello Auntie Kathleen,' I began awkwardly, and then it was suddenly as if Peter was showing me a picture. In my mind I could see him in Auntie Kathleen's front room. There was a haggard, tired-looking Auntie Kathleen holding the phone to her ear and opposite her sat a middle-aged woman wrapped in a warm coat, sipping a cup of tea.

'Oh! Peter's showing me you've got someone with you,' I said.

'Oh yes, I have!' said Auntie Kathleen, 'My friend just popped in.'

Peter began gesticulating towards the woman's feet.

'Something about her shoes . . .' I began, but Peter shook his head and then leant down and tapped the handbag that stood on the floor beside her. 'Oh, not her shoes, her bag,' I corrected myself. It was smart and shiny and a price-tag label appeared on it then disappeared again. I smiled to myself. 'It's a new bag!' I said. 'She's got a brand new bag with her.'

Auntie Kathleen's voice went muffled as she turned away to pass this on to her friend. There was an amazed squawk in the background.

'How did you know?' said Auntie Kathleen, coming back. 'She says she only bought it this morning. How could you know that?'

'Peter told me,' I said. 'Peter's so close to you. He's not gone.'

Then I noticed that Peter was putting his hand up to his throat, and when he did a gold chain appeared there for a second. As his hand touched the chain he glanced at his mother and gave her a look of such pure love it broke my heart that Auntie Kathleen couldn't see it.

'Auntie Kathleen, just one more thing,' I said. 'Peter wants to give you a present. He wants to give you a gold chain.'

He wanted me to mention it and they do say that it's the thought that counts, so I said it out loud, but this seemed rather a pointless message to pass on because how on earth could he do that now?

Yet not long after my call, Auntie Kathleen heard a knock at the door and when she opened it she found her other son Paul standing there. Paul, good-hearted though he was, had never been the sloppy, sentimental type. He was a macho kind of man but for some reason, he said, as he was passing a jeweller's shop in town, he'd got this sudden impulse to go in and buy his mum a gift. Auntie Kathleen opened the little box to find a beautiful gold chain nestling inside.

'Auntie Kathleen found it so comforting,' Mum told me later. 'It made such a difference to her. She's still in pieces, but what you said helped.'

I was pleased, yet this incident made me more confused than ever. I was going through the motions of ordinary life and I was doing well at the care home for people with learning difficulties where I was now working, and yet I kept getting the nagging feeling that I should be doing more.

The sudden death of a young person only a few years older than yourself always brings you up short and makes you re-examine your own life and the path you're treading. But it was as if Peter's death held some special message for me, yet I wasn't sure what it was.

In the end I felt so bruised and tired by the emotional strain that I decided to go away for an early break. I hired a caravan near Tenby for a short seaside holiday with Lisa. It was spring and the sun wasn't yet hot, but small children don't care what the weather's like. Lisa was happy to run about the beach in her little corduroy trousers and sweater making sandpies or kicking through the icy waves with her bare toes, shrieking like a delighted seagull.

It was good to watch such sheer, uncomplicated joy and I could feel myself relaxing. Yet back at the caravan it was a different story. I'd intended to get away to escape him, but somehow I seemed to have brought Peter with me. His presence hung over the whole place. Every time I turned round I expected to see him standing behind me.

'It's time,' I heard him say. 'It's time.'

Time for what? I thought crossly.

Then one evening after I'd put Lisa to bed, I switched on the TV to watch a soap. I moved back to the dralon corner sofa and had just sat down to enjoy the drama when the channel flicked off and re-tuned to a different programme.

Sighing, I got up and flicked it back. But as soon as I sat down the same thing happened again.

The programme that came on appeared to be something about psychics. Impatiently, I turned it over again. I'd had enough of that lot at the spiritualist churches Debbie and Julie used to take me to years ago. I wanted to catch up with the scandals in Albert Square.

But the TV seemed to have a life of its own. Every time I turned it over, it simply turned back.

'Probably only gets one channel out here,' I grumbled to myself. And just to spite it I turned it off altogether. 'I'll look at a magazine,' I said.

So I picked up a magazine, kicked off my shoes and settled down on the sofa to check out the new summer fashions. The next second 'PING' went the TV set and on came the psychic programme again.

'Watch,' said Peter's voice in my ear.

It was crystal clear that Peter wanted me to see this programme, so I gave in and watched. As I'd already gathered from the previous annoying snippets, it was an investigation into psychic events. Several people who believed they were psychic appeared before the camera to describe how they could see people who appeared to be invisible to everyone else, and how they predicted the future or sensed something that was about to happen. Various experts talked about ghosts and how these phenomena might be explained by buildings retaining an imprint of past events in their very bricks and mortar. And, of course, just for balance, a couple of sceptical experts came up with theories as to why the incidents were either all in the mind or just plain con tricks.

I couldn't help noticing that some of the people who thought they were psychic described events very similar to things I'd witnessed myself.

That night I went to bed in an even more unsettled frame of mind, and as I dozed Peter appeared again. It was as if I could see him much more clearly when I was almost asleep.

'It's not for nothing, what you can do,' he said. 'You must use it.'

'I wouldn't know how to begin,' I protested.

'Just begin and you'll learn,' he said. 'It'll come to you. And I'll be here to help.'

And then somehow, just as I did with the Lined Man, I was flying. Peter was beside me and we drifted through the soft clouds out over the ancient stone walls of Tenby town. Down below, the pale horseshoe beach glimmered in the moonlight and then we were speeding away through the darkness over big cities with endless necklaces of lights.

'Down there you'll be known,' said Peter, waving an arm to indicate a vast metropolis. 'And there too,' as we came to another.

It seemed as if we visited a great many places during the night. We zipped across the sea in the blink of an eye and back again, and everywhere we went Peter said I'd work. There were so many places my head began to spin. I'd be worn out for sure if I worked in all that lot, I thought.

Finally, Peter showed me a smart, double-fronted red brick house with a big garden all around it.

'And you'll come here,' he said.

Well, at least that'll be a visit worth making, I thought to myself. I wonder what I'll do there? But before I could get an answer, the picture faded and I was back in bed and falling into a dreamless, exhausted sleep for the rest of the night.

When I woke the next morning I was surprised to find that I felt much more at peace. At some point during the night I must have come to a decision. If I could help people like Auntie Kathleen feel a little bit better I would be glad to do it, I realised, and if all it took was for me to sit back and wait to be shown how, then I'd agree. Like Peter said, I'd get started and find out how to do it afterwards!

There was an odd postscript to the holiday. A few weeks later, talking to Debbie, I discovered that a year or two earlier Peter had enjoyed a break at the very same caravan site just outside Tenby that I'd decided to go to with Lisa, and he'd stayed in the very caravan that I'd been allocated. No wonder I felt his presence so strongly.

Back home, life resumed as hectic as ever. I'd met a new man – a gentle giant called Kevin. Out with Debbie one night I'd got talking to a group of friends in the pub, and with them was a cheerful, easy-going man called Kevin Davis. It wasn't love at first sight, but from then on we kept bumping into each other in the street and stopping for a chat and, somehow, we ended up dating.

Kevin, a carpenter, was good-looking and lean as a greyhound, which was most unfair because he could eat and eat and never put on an ounce. He didn't really believe in psychic things but he was fascinated by my odd skill with everyday objects.

'Here, take my watch,' he'd say, slipping it off his wrist. 'See what you can get!'

And I'd sigh, 'Just this once then,' and I'd shut my eyes for a second. 'You got stuck in traffic today and the car in front of you had a flat tyre and you got out to help . . .'

Kevin would watch me, eyes dancing, half in disbelief, half in wonder.

'You saw me! All right, someone else saw me and told you!' Then he'd laugh and pat my knee, as if I'd caught him out in some clever way he couldn't yet fathom, 'I don't know how you do it girl! But it's a good trick.'

And I'd have to put on a smile and try to hide my frustration. This wasn't quite what Peter had in mind by using my gift I was sure.

Chapter Eleven

I could hear the phone ringing from outside the door. I was standing on the step fumbling for my key with carrier bags of shopping round my feet, and all the time the phone was screaming urgently from inside.

It was probably only someone wanting to sell double glazing or a fitted kitchen, but I rushed in anyway and dived for the receiver like a rugby player.

'Hello!' I gasped breathlessly.

'Oh Diane – thank goodness you're there,' said Julie's voice. 'You've got to help me.'

'Why? What's wrong?' I asked in alarm.

'Oh, nothing serious, but I've got a load of friends coming over for a psychic night and the psychic's not turned up. Can you come and do it?'

'Julie, you've got to be joking,' I said. 'I couldn't do that.'

'Of course you could,' said Julie confidently. 'You're always doing things like that and people always say you're right.'

'I don't think so Julie. I mean, I'm not a proper psychic.'

'Of course you are,' said Julie. 'They all have to start

somewhere. Anyway, it's not serious. Just a bit of fun. Only for twenty minutes or so. And they'll be so disappointed if no-one comes.'

Something about that 'they all have to start somewhere' set bells clanging in my mind. Peter's words 'Just begin and you'll learn . . .' floated back to me. Was this what he meant?

'What would I have to do?' I asked doubtfully.

'Well, the psychic was going to read the tarot cards. Can you do that?'

'Of course not!' I said. 'I mean, I've got a set but I don't know what they mean. I can't read them.'

'That doesn't matter,' said Julie breezily. 'Just waft them about and look mysterious. They'll love it.'

'Julie, I really don't think . . .'

'That's perfect,' Julie went on as if she hadn't heard, 'come at seven and I'll have some vodka or martini, or whatever you like now, ready for you. Help you relax.'

And then she was gone.

I stood there, the phone dangling from my hand, shopping bags sagging round my feet. I'd just got my first booking.

I was petrified when I arrived at Julie's at 7 pm, but her four friends didn't seem the slightest bit worried. As far as they were concerned, I was the stand-in psychic and they gathered round me expectantly.

At a loss, I handed one of them, named Nicola, the tarot cards and let her pick a few out. I laid them in neat lines on the table, like I'd seen them do on the films, but when I turned them over the lurid pictures stared blankly back at me, saying nothing. Before I could panic, Peter arrived at my elbow.

'Look!' he said, and he gestured towards the wall.

It was only a blank wall but as I stared at it I saw the shape of a wedding dress appear and beside it a date was written on a large calendar. As I watched, an unseen hand crossed through the date and the dress seemed to droop sadly.

'You've got a wedding dress ready,' I said to Nicola. 'It's lovely but I can't see you wearing it. I can't see you getting married.'

Nicola did not look best pleased.

'Well, I have got a wedding dress,' she said, 'but I am getting married – next month as it happens – despite what you say.'

I glanced back at the wall. The dress still hung forlornly on its hanger.

'I hope you do if that's what you want,' I said, 'but I can see the date coming and then going and the dress is still hanging up. You're not wearing it.'

This was probably not what Nicola wanted to hear and she moved away to talk to Julie, but the other girls were luckier. When the next one sat down I saw an old woman walk across the wall and smile at the young woman in the chair.

'That's my grand-daughter, that is!' she said proudly.

And when I described her to Julie's friend she was amazed.

'Yes, that's exactly how my gran used to look,' she said.

The evening took a more positive turn. Abandoning the tarot pack, which was obviously no use to me, and opting instead for the blank wall which seemed to act as a sort of psychic cinema screen on which picture symbols appeared, I told the other girls details of boyfriends and husbands and children, which they assured me were quite correct. Nicola, of course, smiled a bit grudgingly. Well, you can't win them all, I thought as I went home.

Yet a month later I got an excited call from Julie.

'Wow, Di – you're so right!'

'What d'you mean?' I asked.

'Remember that Nicola, at my place? The one with the wedding dress? You said she wouldn't get married?'

'Yes,' I said warily.

'Well, I've just heard. The wedding's off! I'm not sure what's gone wrong. I haven't got all the details yet, but apparently Nicola's furious.'

'I bet she is,' I said. 'And it was such a lovely dress an'all. But you know what? Tell her not to be upset. It's for the best. She wouldn't have been happy.'

Julie was torn between sympathy for Nicola and excitement for me.

'Everyone's talking about you, Di. I can get you loads of bookings. All my friends would like a reading.'

'Well, okay Julie, but not too fast,' I said. 'I'm just getting used to this.'

'Why don't you have a chat to Jeff?'

'Who's Jeff?' I asked.

'He's the psychic who didn't turn up,' said Julie. 'I'm sure he'll give you plenty of tips.'

'D'you think he would? Wouldn't I be a sort of rival?'

'Of course not,' said Julie. 'There are not enough psychics to go round.'

I wasn't convinced, but as I thought it over I felt Peter move close to me.

'He can help you,' he said. 'Phone him.'

So I phoned Jeff Marsh and Jeff seemed rather concerned to hear what I'd been up to.

'You should get qualified if you want to do what you've been doing,' he said a little sternly. 'Otherwise you could get yourself into all sorts of trouble.'

'Really?' I asked in horror. I had no idea I might have been doing anything wrong. 'How do I get qualified?' It wasn't as if I'd heard of any 'A' levels or college courses in psychic studies.

Jeff laughed. 'I've recently opened a church called the Rugged Cross,' he said, 'where we nurture young talents. Why don't you come along?'

'Okay,' I said a little doubtfully. I thought of all those stuffy meetings in the old-fashioned spiritualist church my sister and friends used to take me to. I couldn't imagine being involved in anything like that.

But Jeff's group was a pleasant surprise. Young and lively, they met in a cheerful community centre and Jeff, an easy-going man with grey hair tied back in a pony tail, jeans and a leather waistcoat strolled around dispensing advice and devising psychic exercises for everyone.

Sometimes he would discreetly scribble a picture on a small piece of paper, fold it up tightly and then ask everyone to concentrate, try to visualise the sketch and reproduce it for themselves.

I sat in on a session. When I concentrated, the outline of a child's idea of a boat with pointy ends and a triangular sail jumped into my mind and I carefully drew it out. A few minutes later Jeff came round and looked over my shoulder. Then he smiled and unfolded his picture. A boat almost identical to my own looked back at me.

I joined the group and soon made a lot of new friends. It was wonderful to meet other people who were so similar to me and who understood what I was talking about. Little by little Jeff helped me to recognise that it was okay to see spirits, plenty of people could do it, but that standing up on a podium as a medium was a great responsibility.

'You have to remember that you'll be standing up there in front of all these people and every one of them is going to want a message from their loved ones. Yet you're not going to be able to talk to them all. You've got to deal with that. You've also got to realise that communicating in this way takes an enormous amount of energy. Your energy – and you'll be very drained afterwards.'

He made it sound so daunting that he put the fear of God in me. In fact, the first time I stood up like that in front of a crowd I took a couple of Anadins beforehand in a vague attempt to insulate my brain from excess drainage.

Jeff explained that everyone has psychic power to

some extent and the more they use it the more it grows. Yet just as some people can draw a bit while others turn out to be Picasso and Monet, so some people have more psychic ability than others. And when you're highly psychic you're like a radio that's continually turned on; always receiving a signal from somewhere. Interesting, perhaps, but exhausting too unless you can find the off button to give yourself some peace and quiet.

'All you need to do to take a break is to tell the spirits to go away for a while,' said Jeff. 'You may need to repeat that request a couple of times, or ask your guide to help, but they will move away. Oh, and yes, everyone has a guide. Even people who don't realise they're psychic. Many people have several guides.'

Instantly I realised that I knew at least one of my guides – the Lined Man – who'd been there for me for as long as I could remember.

'Sometimes, of course,' Jeff went on, 'you'll want to turn that signal back on to do a reading for someone. All you have to do is "tune in" – that is just concentrate on the person in front of you and automatically you will start receiving information for them or about them. It takes practice, but after a while you'll be able to do it at will. And everyone does it their own way. Some psychics see pictures, others hear voices. It doesn't matter how you do it as long as you're honest and tell the truth. Sometimes when you're working with someone it's difficult to pick up their signal. When in difficulty always ask your guide for help and it'll come.'

Jeff was also very scathing about Ouija boards. He

strongly advised us all never to use them. Apparently they attract the attention of sad or bad spirits who have not crossed into the spirit world but stayed behind, either out of confusion or desire to cause mischief. Once invited into a person's house through the board, they may decide to stay and cause trouble.

Jeff was sometimes helped by a fascinating lady who was called Jan Bird – because of her great love for birds. She strode about chain-smoking and encouraging us to try to give each other messages.

'D'you know, Jan,' I said to her one evening, 'I think you're going to meet a younger man, a *much* younger man – and he's really dark and handsome.'

Jan exploded in laughter. 'I wish!' she said. But funnily enough a few months later she fell for a gorgeous young Turkish fellow half her age and enjoyed a very happy relationship.

After I'd had a few weeks with the group, Jeff seemed to think I was ready to have a crack at tackling the general public. He was putting on a charity evening and asked if I'd like to be one of the psychics. The event was being held in a room in a pub and I decided to donate whatever money came my way to the children's ward of the local hospital.

Once again I was very nervous, but the presence of the other experienced psychics had a calming effect. Unlike most of them, I had no reputation at stake; people's expectation of me was not high, so I could just relax and enjoy myself. At the beginning I was probably the least popular psychic there, but as the evening wore on word spread from the few people who'd ended up at my table because the others were busy, and soon I had quite a queue.

I remember one lady in particular – she must have been in her seventies. She had tight grey curls and a brisk, no-nonsense manner. She sat down quickly on the edge of the chair and looked as if she was about to check her watch. Perhaps she had a bus to catch.

'Okay love, let's get on with it. Let's see what you can do,' she said, folding up her gloves and putting them in her bag.

'Well,' I said, a little put off, and then I stopped. My eyes were drawn not by her face but by the blank wall opposite just as they had been at Julie's party. I saw a removal van parked outside a house and the woman in front of me was standing in front of it. 'I get the impression you're going to be moving house soon.'

The woman laughed scornfully. 'Move house? At my age? I could never see me moving from here. It's not gonna happen. You're wrong there, love.'

I sighed. This was not a good start, but then her father walked into the picture and stood right beside her shoulder. He turned and looked at me and he seemed to want me to know that she'd definitely be moving. I couldn't hear his voice out loud, but the information was going straight into my mind.

'Well, I've got a link with your father . . .' I explained.

'Oh really!' she laughed again. 'In that case, if you're linking with my father you'd better describe him to me.'

I looked over at her dad. He grinned and gestured

towards his feet, half covered by the turn-ups on his trousers. 'He's got turn-ups on his trousers,' I said, 'and black brogues and he's wearing a grey jumper that was knitted for him by his mother.'

The smile faded from the woman's face. 'Oh my gosh!' she said in shock. 'Oh my gosh, you really are linking with my father, aren't you? Everything you said is true.'

All at once her attitude changed completely and she became incredibly enthusiastic.

'Do you realise what you can do with this, love? It's unbelievable.'

'Is it?' I said, a little confused. 'I'm just saying what I can see.'

'But can't you see how clever you are, love? It's amazing. I must tell my friends. Do you have a card or something?'

I laughed, 'No. Not yet. But I'll write my phone number down for you.'

She went off in a very different mood from when she arrived and funnily enough, a few months later, she phoned to tell me that although she'd never have believed it possible, she was actually moving; just as I'd predicted.

'It's unbelievable, love,' she said happily. 'That was the one thing you said that I was sure you'd got wrong!'

The charity evening seemed to be a success and I earned a big bag of money. I was thrilled. I went into town and bought six of the new DVD players that had just come out, along with dozens of DVDs to go with them. Then I picked up an armful of the latest Playstation games and a pile of other trinkets that caught my eye and staggered off to the hospital with them. I walked into the children's ward like Father Christmas and I couldn't have arrived at a more opportune moment.

'We've just had our video machines stolen,' said the sister incredulously, as she opened box after box of new DVD players, 'so we couldn't put any films on for the children. These are exactly what we need.'

I don't know who was more delighted, her or me. It gave me a fantastic, warm feeling to be able to make them so happy. I was beginning to see just how useful this gift could be. No wonder Peter wanted me to get out there and use it.

I threw myself into Jeff's nurturing evenings with more enthusiasm now that I understood the potential, and I soon discovered another facet to this strange ability.

As my confidence grew I plucked up the courage to take a table at a Psychic Fair. I was still a new face and the woman who booked the event looked a bit doubtful when I applied.

'We only provide the table,' she said, 'so I take it you'll be bringing all your things with you.'

'Things?' I asked, a bit worried. 'What things?'

The woman gave me an: oh-dear-is-this-all-going-to-be-a-big-mistake? kind of look. 'Most people bring their posters and photographs, backboards or any displays they use. Stands and shelves and so on. And obviously their crystal balls or tarot cards or whatever they prefer.'

I suddenly felt hopelessly amateur.

'Um . . . well, I haven't got anything like that,' I said.

She shrugged. 'Well, it's up to you of course,' she said witheringly, 'but it's important to have a good image. That's what the others bring, and you won't make much impression if you don't.'

I sighed. It was too late to start putting together a mini-stage set now, even if I could afford it, which I couldn't, so I would just have to stick to what I knew. I took a nice clean pink sheet off my bed, ironed it carefully and on the day of the fair I spread it out on my table. As the other psychics unfolded their shelves, drawing-pinned their displays and stood various mystic cut-outs around their stands, I filled a vase with water and stuck a bunch of pink and white roses into it. Then I placed the flowers neatly in the centre of my tablecloth and that was it. I was done. I sat down on my folding chair amid all the hammering, banging and frenetic activity to wait.

The organiser was walking up and down the aisles inspecting the stands as they took shape. The hall was awash with black velvet and silver swirls, misty planets and banks of crystals. The faint scent of incense began to uncoil through the air. When she got to my table the organiser stopped.

'Is that it?' she asked.

'Well – yes,' I admitted.

She frowned. 'It's a bit spartan, isn't it?'

'Well, I thought the roses . . .'

'Yes, the roses are very nice,' said the woman, 'but haven't you got a crystal ball or something?'

I shook my head. 'I'm afraid I don't use one,' I said apologetically.

She sighed. 'It's not exactly atmospheric, is it? Oh well, I s'pose it's too late now. But visuals are very important dear. Have you done one of these fairs before?'

I shook my head again.

'I thought not. Oh well. Good luck.' And losing interest she went off to admire the heavily atmospheric table next door.

As usual I got off to a slow start, but after a few customers had walked away professing amazement, something of a buzz began to build in the hall. More and more people stopped at my table and it wasn't long before I had quite a queue.

I was getting used to doing readings by now and here at the fair they were falling into the familiar pattern when a woman called June Davis sat down. She was a friendly, smiling lady with a calm, open face and I expected to make contact with a mother or father or some aged relative. Instead there was nothing but a terrible pain in my back. Involuntarily my hand flew round to my spine.

'Oh!' I said in surprise. 'My back really, really hurts.'

June's eyes widened. 'That's right,' she said.

The pain subsided for me, but I knew that for June it was still there and my heart went out to her. Peter stepped from nowhere to explain in my ear what was wrong.

'Your discs are completely worn,' I said, 'and you've had operations and physiotherapy and lots of treatments, but your back still hurts.'

'That's true,' June agreed. 'Unfortunately there's nothing else they can do now.'

But I hardly took in what she was saying because I was distracted by a strange sensation in my hands. They were tingling and filling with heat. My palms and fingers were getting hotter and hotter until they were almost burning. It was quite uncomfortable and I felt as if the only way to stop them exploding was to place them on June's back. This could be embarrassing, but I had to ask.

'June,' I said, 'this has never happened to me before but my hands are getting really hot and I feel as if I want to put them on your back. Would you mind?'

'Why not?' said June. 'I've tried everything else!'

I had no idea how you do healing or how long it takes, but June sat forward on her chair and I came round and laid my blazing palms on the small of her back. I stood there like that for a while, the heat steaming out of my skin.

'You know, I can feel it getting hot now,' said June in surprise after a few minutes, 'but it's not unpleasant.'

Then the heat began to fade and I took this as a sign that whatever needed to happen had happened. My hands dropped to my sides and the skin resumed its normal temperature.

'Well,' I said, going back round to my side of the table. 'I don't exactly know what happened there but hopefully it's helped a bit.'

June gathered her bag and jacket. 'You never know,' and she started to get up, stiffly at first and then unexpectedly fluid. A strange look crossed her face. She pulled herself upright and took a couple of steps. She twisted her hips slightly one way and then the other. And then she beamed.

'I feel fine!' she said. 'I don't know what you did but my back doesn't hurt. That's incredible. It's nearly time for my next painkiller, but I don't think I'll bother.'

I was delighted. 'You mean you think it helped?'

'I'm sure it did,' said June. 'I was in agony when I walked in here. One of the reasons why I came to your table was for a sit down! How long d'you think this will last?'

'I've no idea,' I said, just as bewildered as June. 'Give me a ring and let me know how you get on.'

By the end of the fair I think the organiser was willing to concede that visuals weren't quite as vital as she originally believed. I had just as many visitors to my spartan table, and possibly more, than the elaborate edifices all around me.

Several months later I heard from June again.

'Can you give me another session, Diane?' she asked when she phoned. 'What you did at the fair lasted six months, but I overdid it the other day and my back's started twanging again. Could I book a top-up?'

Since then June has been back several times for a

top-up, which seems to work better than her painkillers ever did, and there's the added advantage that there's no danger of side effects and it's cheap. I made up my mind there and then that I couldn't possibly charge for healing. The National Health Service is free, after all, because we believe that lack of money shouldn't prevent people from receiving medical care, and that's how I feel about my healing. I've stuck to that decision ever since.

Chapter Twelve

I liked the house immediately. It was an older-style terraced home in a quiet part of town and as soon as you walked in the front door you were enveloped in a warm, loving atmosphere.

It was a Tardis of a house. Much bigger inside than it looked from the outside, thanks to a large extension that had been added on the back. There was a second, inner hall that led to a spacious sitting room and a smart separate dining room. The whole place was beautifully decorated in the latest fashionable shades of green and pink.

As I walked into the back sitting room I got the impression of an old lady ensconced on a chair, knitting. She smiled up at me over her wool and although she didn't speak, she somehow gave me to understand that this was the treasured home of her nephew and his wife, who had sadly lavished so much money on doing it up that they could no longer afford to live in it.

'Let's buy it!' I said to Kevin. And that's exactly what we did. But throughout our time there, much as I loved it, I never felt that house in Clare Street really belonged to us. It was as if we were merely caring for it until its rightful owners came back.

Kevin and I seemed to have made our relationship permanent. He spent so much time at the flat with Lisa and me that it seemed only sensible to move to a bigger place together. One of these days, we assumed, we'd probably get married, but I was in no hurry to repeat the experiment and besides, there was a strange little feeling in the back of my mind that I'd never be Mrs Davis. No matter how I tried to peer into the future and see myself as Kevin's wife, the picture just wouldn't come. I was beginning to trust my instincts now and if I couldn't see something, I'd learned it wasn't going to happen. Why it wasn't going to happen, though, was still a mystery to me. But I had no wish to probe more deeply. For the time being we were happy, and I decided to leave it at that.

My job in social services had continued to go well and the clients still fascinated me. I was working now with adults with severe behavioural problems and my psychic abilities came in very useful. I was rarely taken by surprise by unpredictable tantrums and because of this I was always able to cope.

One hefty young woman named Sally kept all the staff on their toes. She often acted like a furious, overgrown two-year-old, and on one occasion she rampaged through the home smashing everything in her path and hurling heavy items right through the windows. When order was finally restored the crockery was replaced with plastic cups, saucers and tableware and the windows were mended with safety glass.

Sally didn't realise this at first and having enjoyed her

spree immensely, a few weeks later she attempted a repeat performance. This time she was disappointed to find that objects just bounced off the windowpanes and cups and saucers rolled harmlessly across the floor. Once it finally sank in that nothing was going to break, Sally gave up throwing things around. It was no fun any more.

I started tuning in to Sally and I soon realised that she herself had a powerful sixth sense. She picked up on people's energies and she either liked or disliked them on sight. If she detected the tiniest shiver of fear in a member of staff she exploited it cruelly.

Realising this, I always stood up to her. Sally had recently discovered that it upset people tremendously if she bit them, so she charged around in a threatening manner, baring her teeth and making the most of the excitement as terrified residents scattered in all directions.

'Okay, Sally,' I'd tell her, barring her path. 'If you want to bite me, come on and bite me. Help yourself. And then we're going back to your room.'

And Sally would laugh as if such a thought never entered her head and would happily walk back with me to watch TV.

One memorable day Margaret, one of the senior members of staff, went on a course to learn novel new techniques of handling troublesome clients. When she came back she was full of amazement at what she'd been told.

'It's the opposite of what we've been taught up till

now, Di,' she said. 'They say we should try acting like our residents. Do what they do.'

'Do what they do?' I said in surprise. Well, it sounded an intriguing theory. Could it possibly work? 'Okay. Shall we give it a go?'

Margaret was sceptical that it would have any effect, but she was as intrigued as me.

'Why not?' she laughed.

So we went into the sitting room where the assorted residents were gathered, chatting, watching TV, or wandering about as usual. They looked up expectantly as we walked in, but they were in for a shock.

'Did you take my biscuit Margaret?' I shrieked suddenly.

'No!' Margaret shrieked back.

'You did!' I yelled and promptly made a run at her. Margaret skipped away and jumped onto the sofa just as Sally so often did, and I leapt after her.

As the residents watched open-mouthed, Margaret and I, shouting at the tops of our voices, bounced on the sofa like a trampoline and then leapt from armchair to armchair screaming. It was like being a naughty toddler again and felt strangely liberating.

But of course the residents didn't like it one bit. They cowered away from us as if they feared we'd gone completely mad and the effect on Sally was remarkable. As the other residents backed away in alarm, Sally, who was so accustomed to producing this effect herself, didn't know how to react. She hesitated for a moment, staring at us in disapproval, then she marched in front of her fellows and stood there protecting them.

After a couple more moments of mayhem, Margaret and I felt we'd probably gone far enough. We calmed down and agreed to climb off the sofa, and to our astonishment Sally transformed herself into a responsible adult before our eyes. Once she was confident that we'd got over our brainstorm, she shepherded the residents back to their chairs like a caring member of staff, and then went to fetch them soothing cups of water. I'd never seen anything like it.

'That's incredible, Margaret. It works,' I said. All the same, I didn't know what the council would think of their staff behaving even worse than the disturbed people in their care. 'But I'm not sure we should try it again!'

We never did.

Although it was hard work, I enjoyed it, yet as the months went on I found it increasingly difficult to cope with the physical demands of the job. I was plagued by terrible stomach pains. I didn't realise it at the time but my endometriosis was getting much worse and other problems were developing. I contacted the endometriosis society for advice and went backwards and forwards to the doctor. I tried to heal myself by focusing on the pain and willing it to go away, but every time I tried the Lined Man came close and told me that I needed to go to hospital for an operation. There seem to be some complaints that respond to natural healing and others that require conventional medical treatment, and it seemed I'd got one of the latter. The trouble was, my doctor didn't seem to agree. I was sent for several medical tests but nothing seemed conclusive.

At times I was in tears with the pain and Debbie actually took me to casualty on a couple of occasions when I almost collapsed in agony when we were out. Yet I was always sent away with a couple of paracetamol and the suggestion that I must be suffering from stress.

I was off sick so much that in the end I decided to give up my job to concentrate on looking after Lisa and Kevin and getting myself well. If I really was suffering stress then perhaps an extended period of calm living would cure it. The one thing I could still manage though, was my psychic work, which could normally be done sitting down.

Ever since my success with June and her bad back, an endless stream of people had found their way to my door. One wealthy man brought his wife to me twice a week in the hope that she might be able to go away with him on holiday. They dearly wanted to visit Tenerife but the poor woman had such pain in her hips she couldn't sit down for the duration of the flight, so foreign holidays were out.

While the man sat outside in his big Jag, I gave the woman healing in our dining room, which I'd commandeered as my 'clinic' owing to its quiet position at the back of the house and its tranquil decoration of soft pinks. It took a few sessions but it wasn't long before the wife's pain had subsided so much that they were able to fly off abroad for the first time in years.

Word spread and the next thing I knew I was being

sent a policeman who'd broken his foot and was still off work because it wouldn't mend properly. He too was soon on his way again, much recovered.

I remained just as puzzled as my patients as to how it was that they improved when I gave them healing, but I was thrilled when it obviously worked. I began to form the impression that from the other side Peter was shaping me into a sort of psychic osteopath, because so far all my patients had been suffering from bone and joint problems. Then one day a beautiful girl called Samantha came for a reading. She had long blonde hair, expertly applied make-up and such style and confidence that I thought she must be a model. She sat down and folded herself up in an 'I-don't-intend-to-give-anything-away' sort of posture and waited for me to tell her her future.

Almost immediately her mother Margaret was at her side and so much love flowed out towards Samantha that I got the impression Margaret, who was a comparatively young woman, had died in order that her daughter should live. Margaret began banging on her chest and gesturing towards Samantha, and as she did so my body started to ache all over and my lungs hurt.

'You've got problems with your chest,' I said, 'and your mum used to bang your back to help you breathe. You still have to have your back rubbed every morning. Your mum took you to hospital so many times and she even took you to see a famous healer when you were a tiny little girl. Mathew Manning it was. You would have died if you hadn't seen him.'

Samantha stared at me open-mouthed. 'That's amazing,' she said. 'I've got cystic fibrosis. I've been to loads of psychics but no-one's ever picked that up before. And I've not even so much as coughed in front of you.'

'Your mother says that when you were feeling poorly she used to brush your hair. It soothed you to have your hair brushed. She used to brush away for hours.'

Samantha nodded.

'Oh and she's pleased because you've just got engaged.'

Samantha laughed, opened her handbag and took out a sparkling ring.

'I might as well put it back on now,' she said. 'I hid it so you wouldn't get any clues!'

At the time I'd never even heard of cystic fibrosis, but it was clear Samantha was worried that the condition might be life threatening.

'I see you going on and on,' I said. 'You can tell that fiance of yours you've got years in you yet.'

And as I said the words I got an impression of a crowd of young people standing around Samantha, of all shapes and sizes – some of them quite small children. I realised that these were the patients she'd met in hospital over the years, the ones that hadn't made it.

Samantha was very pleased with her reading and before she left she let me give her healing.

As soon as I put my hands on her shoulders I could feel a dreadfully tight feeling in my chest and it was difficult to breathe. Momentarily I always feel some of my patients' symptoms and my hands always become so hot it's as if they're going to burn unless I transfer some of the energy to the sick person in front of me. I never know how long this will take but I can tell when I've done enough because the heat goes out of my palms and they revert to their normal temperature.

'That feels fabulous,' said Samantha afterwards as she gathered up her bag, 'it's so relaxing. Can I bring some of my friends another time?'

'Of course you can,' I said.

That must have been nearly fifteen years ago. Samantha is now around 38 years old and whenever she feels unwell she has more healing. Her lungs have only about 28 per cent capacity and yet she still manages to lead a happy life. The doctors are amazed. They think she's a walking miracle.

The sad thing was that when Samantha brought three other young CF patients to me I was unable to see very much for them. I tried and tried to peer ahead, to picture them in the years after college, but no images came. I shrugged if off at the time. It obviously doesn't work with everyone, I told myself. But over the next few years each one of those other girls tragically died. Gradually it began to dawn on me that the reason I couldn't see their futures was because they didn't have futures. Not here on this side anyway.

The Ouija board craze continued to grip the area and one day I popped in to see my neighbour Angela and found her there with her twin sister Gaynor, both happily playing what they thought of as a game.

The Lined Man had explained to me that Ouija boards were dangerous, particularly in untrained hands, because they encouraged lost or mischievous spirits to enter a house, so I never joined in. Peter too had made it clear that he disapproved as much as the Lined Man, so I was amazed to see on this occasion that Peter was standing beside Gaynor as she leaned over the board, finger resting lightly on the glass.

Peter glanced up at me and then gestured to the space on the other side of Gaynor. As I tried to work out what he meant, my eyes began to take in the shape of another young man standing there, a slim, dark-haired fellow with very blue eyes and a gentle smile. There was something about the way he stood, with his body half shielding Gaynor, that looked protective and he was clearly very fond of her.

'He took himself over,' said Peter. 'That's why he needs some help. But he's protecting her from any harm from this silly game.'

'Gaynor, did you know a young man with dark hair and blue eyes – who died not long ago?' I asked.

'Why yes,' said Gaynor, 'I had a friend like that who committed suicide. It was so sad. He was such a lovely boy.'

'Well, he's come back to look after you,' I said. Which I think Gaynor found rather reassuring.

I still managed to work at charity evenings from time to time and one night, when I was back in the room over the pub where I'd first trained with Jeff, I had a very strange experience.

People who didn't know me still tended to approach my table in a grudging way, as if they thought I was trying to con them, but the lady who sat down in front of me now had a friendly, open smile that reflected her open mind.

'I'm Vicki,' she said.

I liked her immediately, but as I began to tune in I was astonished to see Peter appear looking especially handsome in full dress uniform, his hair glowing like gold.

Now, of course, I often saw Peter when I was working because he helped me to sort out the messages, but this time it was clear he hadn't come for my benefit but for Vicki's. He stood beside her and tried to put his arm round her, and next to him were two little babies.

It was unbelievable. I didn't know what to make of it. I expect my mouth opened and shut like a landed fish.

'Good God,' I said, 'I've got my cousin Peter standing beside you as if he knows you. And he's trying to show me two babies.'

Vicki turned a little pale. 'Peter? I used to have a boyfriend called Peter George. It was years ago. He was my first love. It all went wrong and then I found out I was pregnant. I had a termination but they didn't realise I was carrying twins. Later on I lost the other one as well. I had no idea he was your cousin.'

'And I had no idea about you!' I said.

It was an astonishing evening.

Julie still put me in touch with friends who wanted private readings and sometimes they passed my number on. Most of the time this was fine, but at one house I went to I had a bit of a scare.

I didn't know the woman who'd invited me round but she wanted readings for herself and a couple of friends. It was a perfectly normal house in a perfectly normal street but as I walked up the path to the front door I began to feel a little wobbly. I put it down to the fact I might be starting a cold and knocked on the door.

Almost immediately, a tall woman with long, reddish hair flung it open.

'You must be Diane,' she said in a pleasant enough voice. But for a second I couldn't speak. My eyes were riveted to the necklace that showed through the V of her blouse. It was a chunky, silvery symbol of some kind and just the sight of it sent strange shivers down my spine.

'Yes,' I croaked, my voice cracking. 'Sorry. I think I'm getting a cold.'

'Never mind. Come in, Diane.'

And she led me into the house. It wasn't over-bright inside but it wasn't eerily dark either, yet somehow I could feel deep shadows all about me and it was difficult to see. I had the strangest sensation that I was under water and I could hardly breathe. My arms and legs felt heavy and dragged down as if I was wading through a thick, sluggish lake.

'Are you okay, Diane?' someone asked.

'Yes,' I said automatically. But an icy cold draught was making me shiver and my head was beginning to spin. 'Actually no. No – I'm not.'

I felt terrible. I thought I must be having some sort of panic attack.

'I'm so sorry,' I said, 'I've got to go. I'm not going to be able to read for you tonight after all. I think I'm ill.'

There were sympathetic murmurings all around but I couldn't properly see who was speaking. I rushed for the door and bolted out into the fresh air, my heart racing. I must have the flu coming, I thought, as I walked thankfully away down the street. But strangely, the more I walked, the better I felt. By the time I got home all the symptoms had disappeared and I was fine. It was difficult to believe I'd got over flu so quickly and throughout the next couple of days I kept half-expecting the virus to strike properly, but I remained totally sniffle free.

It was all very puzzling. I wondered if I should make a new appointment with the woman I'd let down, but I realised I had no desire to return to that house ever again. Then a few weeks later I bumped into a stranger in the street. I didn't know her but she evidently knew me.

'We met at Nerys's house, don't you remember?' she said. 'That night you couldn't do the reading – you were ill.'

'Oh yes. I remember,' I said.

'I know the real reason why you couldn't do readings in that house,' she said.

'You do?' I said in surprise.

'Yes. It wasn't because you were ill. It was because she's a witch.'

My eyes bulged. 'A witch?'

The woman nodded, 'Oh, I don't think she practises black magic. Strictly white, I hear. But that's probably why you couldn't do anything.'

'Probably,' I agreed weakly.

You certainly saw all walks of life in this job, I reflected as I carried my shopping back to the car. I hadn't really believed there were still witches until that moment but I could totally believe it now.

And the unusual experiences kept on coming. One night I was lying on my bed having a rest when I turned my head and saw an elderly man standing in the bedroom. I knew he was a spirit person because of the silent and abrupt way he'd appeared, but there was nothing menacing about him even though he looked rather unusual. He had thick, long white hair that flowed past his shoulders, a tanned face and a strong hawk-like nose. He looked exactly like an American Indian except for the fact he was wearing an ordinary T-shirt rather than a tunic and feathered head-dress. He was holding a large black book and he appeared to want to lecture me.

'I'm here to teach you patience,' he said. 'You're not listening to me.'

Which was a little unfair since he'd only just arrived and this was the first I'd heard of it.

'I'm trying to listen to you,' I said.

'Now this is a bison, can you see that?' he said, holding up a picture briefly then snatching it away, 'and this is a buffalo, can you see this?' and on and on he went, flashing endless pictures of birds and animals before my tired eyes. I was starting to get a bit bored.

'Who are you anyway?'

'Pay attention. And this is a rattle snake . . .'

I sighed. If he wouldn't tell me who he was I didn't want to work with him. I had enough mystery visitors as it was. The Lined Man, even after all these years, still avoided telling me his name and it was immensely frustrating.

'You're meeting my grandson tomorrow,' the American Indian said unexpectedly.

I turned back quickly, 'Am I? Who is he?'

But the old man just shook his white head. 'Patience,' he said and faded away.

I flopped back on the bed in irritation. Perhaps I dozed off, but the next minute, it seemed, the phone was ringing. It was my friend Mary.

'Diane this is very hush-hush but d'you think you could come over tomorrow and do a reading for a friend of ours?'

'I expect so,' I said. 'Who is it?'

'Well, keep it really quiet. My husband is working on a documentary for television and he's interviewing this real Indian chief called Sitting Bull. That's his real name. He's staying with us and we thought it would be really interesting to see what you pick up.'

All sleepiness instantly evaporated.

'Sitting Bull?'

'Yes, really. Sitting Bull,' said Mary.

'I'd be delighted,' I said, quite excited, 'I think it will be very interesting indeed.'

Sitting Bull did not disappoint. When I arrived at Mary's the next day I was confronted by one of the most enormous men I've ever seen. He must have been at least 7ft tall. He was dressed in everyday clothes: jeans, a checked shirt and open-toed sandals, and when he sat down he dwarfed the chair. He was so big yet so gentle. I could see vibrant colours flowing all around him and I knew instantly he was a good man.

'Say whatever you see,' he said softly in a strong American accent.

At his voice there was a sound in the room like the faint whir of wings and I had the oddest sense that a giant eagle was slowly circling in the air above us, despite the fact that we were indoors. Then Sitting Bull's grandfather appeared again, still equipped with his book.

'He says he's come to teach,' I explained, after describing the old man and his book.

Sitting Bull nodded. 'My grandfather was a teacher. He spoke very good English and he always carried this big black book everywhere with him.'

As the reading went on more of Sitting Bull's relatives came close. There was one called Night Owl, another called Eagle Owl and various others named after wild things. They talked of how all the relatives would gather round a big table to discuss family matters and make important decisions.

Sitting Bull was very kind and confirmed that

everything I said, no matter how unlikely it seemed to me, was quite correct.

Afterwards, when I'd finished, he said he wanted to show me something. He went off to his room and came back with his suitcase. He opened it up, folded back the lid and I saw that instead of being filled with folded shirts, pairs of socks and underwear as you'd expect, it contained nothing but a pair of horns and a huge black cape.

Sitting Bull shook out the cape. It was made of real bull skin, thick and heavy with a big curly fur cuff at the top and it reached to his feet. When he put it on with the horned head dress he was a formidable sight – all 7ft of him.

Like anyone else going on a journey, Sitting Bull had packed the essentials. And that was what was essential to him.

Later I was touched to see the entry he wrote in Mary's visitors' book: 'Thank you for your time. It really felt as if the room filled with the old people' and it was signed 'Sitting Bull'.

Chapter Thirteen

It was very annoying. My healing practice was going well and people told me I made a big difference to whatever was ailing them, yet I couldn't seem to help myself. I was getting more and more run down by chronic endometriosis and neither the doctors nor my own meditation seemed to make much difference. I closed my eyes and tried to focus on the pain. I imagined myself in a bath of healing blue water, soaking the pain away, dissolving it into nothingness. Yet, although I might feel more relaxed, I couldn't cure the problem. Three weeks out of every four it became quite difficult even to walk and I bought a TENS machine to beat the discomfort. Yet nothing worked and still the Lined Man insisted that an operation was the only answer.

Yet, despite my gynaecological problems, I had a strong feeling that my family wasn't complete. I was going to have another baby – a little boy. When I closed my eyes, I could see him clear as clear – a beautiful child with dark hair and dark eyes, just like mine. I was delighted at the thought of having a son to go with my lovely little daughter. In fact I was so convinced that this new baby would come along, I painted the spare bedroom in blue.

'How would you like a little brother?' I asked Lisa.

'Wouldn't mind,' said Lisa.

And Kevin, who was beginning to come round to the accuracy of my predictions, liked the idea too. However, the months passed and there was no hint of any baby. In fact the possibility of my getting pregnant began to recede alarmingly.

I became more and more unwell. In the end I was so ill the doctor arranged for me to have an endoscopy – they inserted a tiny camera through my belly-button and discovered that I had the worst case of endometriosis they'd ever seen. There was no possibility of conceiving, they told me, I was far too clogged up inside. In fact, the only solution to my problems was an immediate hysterectomy.

I was bitterly disappointed. How could I have been so wrong? I had been quite certain that I was going to have a little boy.

'I'm sorry, Diane, but you must put that idea out of your mind,' said the doctor. 'Concentrate on how much better you're going to feel after the operation. You'll be a new woman.'

And he went on to explain that I'd receive a letter from the hospital shortly, with the date for my operation.

On the way home I gave myself a serious talking to. You're not going to have a child, I told myself. Put it out of your mind. The important thing is to be well and enjoy the child you have. But a rebellious little voice kept coming back to me: 'You're going to have a boy.'

Despite this, I couldn't avoid telling Lisa and Kevin what was going on. They needed to be prepared if I had to go into hospital.

'But I thought you said I was going to have a little brother,' said Lisa in confusion when I explained what the doctor had told me.

'I know, love, I know. I thought I was, but obviously I'm not.'

'So we didn't need to paint the spare room blue then,' said Kevin, trying to jolly me out of my low spirits.

'The stupid thing is, I still think we did,' I couldn't help admitting.

Kevin shook his head in despair at my stubbornness. 'You've got to face facts, Diane.'

'I know. Maybe it'll happen some other way.'

Kevin thought I was clutching at straws and he was probably right. While he liked the idea of a new son, he already had children from a previous marriage, so he didn't feel a desperate need to be a father again and, more than anything, he hated to see me suffering so much. Yet I could still see that beautiful boy in my mind's eye. How could this be? That child was part of my future somehow, I was sure of it, so where was he going to come from? Perhaps we'd adopt him. Once I'd got the operation over with, I thought to myself, I'll have to find out about adoption.

My appointment duly came through and yet still I

couldn't rid myself of the feeling that I was going to have a baby.

'I think I'll just go and have a pregnancy test first,' I said to Kevin a couple of days beforehand.

He looked at me incredulously. 'Don't be so stupid, Diane! That's crazy. You're having a hysterectomy in two days' time.'

'I know,' I said, 'but even so . . .'

Even I was wondering if I was going mad by this time, but I couldn't help myself. The voice in my mind was so insistent I couldn't rest until I'd done everything possible. After Kevin had gone to work and Lisa to school, I took myself off to a local chemist that advertised highly accurate pregnancy tests. I gave my sample and then, too exhausted to go another step, I sat down on the chair beside the counter to wait for the results.

The chemist emerged from behind her little screen holding a scrap of paper but I stayed in the chair, still aching too much to stand up. I was prepared to hear the worst.

'Congratulations, Mrs Lloyd Hughes,' said the chemist, smiling, 'it's positive. You're pregnant.'

For a second I thought I'd misheard. 'I'm sorry . . . ?'

'It's positive,' she repeated.

I'd known, yet I was still amazed. 'There couldn't be any mistake?' I asked, trying not to break into the biggest smile ever. 'You're quite certain?'

'Absolutely certain,' said the chemist. 'You can do it again if you like, but it's highly accurate.'

And suddenly, pain or no pain, I had to leap up and rush straight back to the doctor's. The hysterectomy would have to be cancelled.

For some reason, though, the doctor was not over-joyed at my news. He didn't seem inclined to believe me and even if he was forced to concede that the test was positive he didn't think that it was a good sign.

'With your track record, if you are pregnant it's prob-ably in the fallopian tube, which is very dangerous,' he said. 'You've just got too many problems to expect to have another child. We'll get you a scan to see exactly what's going on, but put all thoughts of having this baby out of your mind.'

How could I put all thoughts of the baby out of my mind? I couldn't think of anything else. I fretted impatiently until the scan the following day, but deep down I was sure everything would be all right and, to the astonishment of the medical staff, it was. The scan revealed a tiny little foetus, safely ensconced in the womb, heart beating strongly. He appeared to be about five weeks old.

The doctor admitted defeat. 'Well, I would never have believed it possible,' he said, 'but the baby looks fine. The pregnancy probably won't be easy, but if you're determined to go ahead I suggest you have the hysterectomy straight after the birth.'

'Anything you say doctor,' I said happily.

I was truly delighted and Kevin was overjoyed. His face lit up when I told him and he gave me a big hug. It seemed like he did want to be a father again after all. I don't think he'd even realised himself how much he wanted this child.

Life didn't get any easier but I knew I was doing the right thing. The doctor had advised me to get as much rest as I could and the only way to do that was to give up my psychic work. In truth it had all become too much for me. Word had spread so far that the phone never stopped ringing and people continually turned up unannounced on the doorstep.

'Oh, please see me,' they'd beg, standing there tearfully in the pouring rain. 'It's taken me three hours to get here and I've lost a son.'

And they looked so sad I didn't have the heart to turn them away. Yet there were only so many hours in the day and I had a family to care for too. I couldn't eat a meal, help Lisa with her homework or sit and watch a TV programme with Kevin without being called away to comfort some distressed person on the phone. The minute I put the phone down it would start ringing again, and quite often someone would be knocking on the door as well.

Many of the cases were genuinely desperate. On several occasions I had to talk people out of committing suicide there and then. Others were disturbing; I lost count of the number of people who believed they were possessed and dialled my number in terror, pleading with me to drive away the demons. I don't know whether it was the effect of drink, drugs or too much meddling with the Ouija board but the calls – some of which went on until three in the morning – left me emotionally drained and exhausted.

Typical was the woman who insisted that while lying alone in bed she could feel a man groping her even though there was no-one there. Whether she was imagining things or not I couldn't say, but I told her to speak to the man and tell him very firmly to go away and he would. A couple of days later she called again to say that my advice seemed to have worked. I was pleased, of course, but hoped that would be the last I heard from her.

I had no energy spare to give to Kevin and Lisa and I began to feel so torn. Kevin was getting resentful and who could blame him? Why should he feel guilty about wanting a little attention from his partner? And poor Lisa must have begun to assume she always came second, ever behind the next distraught stranger who seemed to need her mum more than she did.

It wasn't fair to either of them and I was beginning to feel I couldn't cope any more. I wanted my own life back. I wanted to be Diane the mother.

'I'm sorry,' I said to the Lined Man and to Peter when they moved in to talk to me, 'I can't do this any more. I can't handle it. You'll have to stop.'

But, of course, they were there before me. They knew how I was feeling and that I needed a break.

'Do what you must do,' said the Lined Man. 'I'm always here for you and you never stop learning. Learn whenever you can. Nothing's wasted.'

I pondered his words long afterwards. I felt that even

if I gave up doing personal readings, I needed to understand a lot more about the theory of psychic matters. I began reading books and a friend gave me the works of a medium called Betty Shine. I hadn't heard of her before but as I learned more of her life story I realised that I had come across many of the things she talked about.

'My God. I'm just like that Betty,' I thought in surprise.

Many of the books advised frequent sessions of meditation and gave step by step instructions on how to do it. It wasn't difficult and I found it very helpful. I badly needed to relax and I found that once I started meditating I began to discover several guides who were helping me. When I closed my eyes and cleared my mind of busy thoughts I could easily visualise the Lined Man, who seemed to be becoming more venerable and distinguished by the week and was developing a long beard and flowing white robes. Then there was Peter, more of a companion and confidant to me, and finally there was a changing cast of other people who appeared to drop in casually from time to time. One of them was an Indian, but not Sitting Bull's teacher grandfather. I think he'd given me up as a bad job after failing to make me grasp 'patience'.

Outwardly it may have appeared that little was happening, but inside, although I hardly realised it, I was continuing to work on my gift. It was very difficult to turn people away when they arrived at the door, and often I relented and let them in, but I told Julie and my other 'regulars' to spread the word that I'd given up and gradually the message got through. Peace returned to Clare Street.

Liam was born on September 15 1994, and he was just as beautiful as his sister had been. He was dark haired and dark eyed, as I'd known he would be. The surgeon gave me a few weeks to recover from the difficult birth and then I was whisked back for a hysterectomy. When they opened me up they were amazed to discover a large but benign tumour on the bowel which had been adding to the pressure and discomfort of the endometriosis. No wonder I was complaining of pain.

It was a great relief to have my medical problems finally sorted out, but it was frustrating to go home to my newborn baby, unable to lift him or run up and down stairs when he cried. For several weeks after the operation I wasn't allowed to drive or even hoover the floor and the most I could manage was changing a nappy or a bit of bottle feeding.

Kevin was marvellous with his new son. He would walk around with the baby on his shoulder and Liam reclined happily like a tiny Elvis Presley with his black hair scuffed up in a little quiff.

And perhaps to compensate for my lack of physical ability, I developed a knack of being able to tune in to Liam mentally. If he woke up crying and I was downstairs, I would concentrate very hard on the cot where he lay and send comforting thoughts to surround him. Within moments everything would go quiet.

It worked like magic, but woe betide me if I let my concentration waver. Several times I'd just got Liam off to sleep in this way when the phone would ring. I'd start chatting, forget myself and a few minutes later lonely yells would start erupting from the blue nursery.

'You're not concentrating!' Kevin would hiss. And I'd have to come off the phone and set my mind to transmitting soothing waves upstairs again. Almost immediately the yells faded into silence.

It made me smile the way Kevin reacted. From being a sceptic who viewed my abilities as little more than a party trick, he was now completely convinced that I exercised some sort of remote hold over the baby. Whenever Liam acted up, Kevin expected me to work a miracle and, strangely enough, it seemed as if I could. With just concentration and the application of my mind I was able to get Liam to sleep for five hours at a time – long enough for me to get the rest I needed to recover from my operation.

'You ought to write a book on baby care!' joked Julie one day when she saw the technique in action.

I suspected I had some unseen helpers on my side too. Sometimes when I went to check on Liam I'd hear happy gurgles coming from his room and I'd walk in to see an old woman leaning over his cot, playing with him. She had a large, cuddly frame, round face and white wavy hair. I assumed it was the old auntie who used to live in the house. Whoever she was, Liam loved her.

Week by week I grew stronger and I adored being at

home with my two children. As well as communicating with Liam telepathically I was able to help Lisa with her homework. If any little tests appeared on the horizon I was able to tune in and find out what subjects she needed to revise. If there was a lesson that was proving difficult I could ask my guides to explain it to me so that I could find the right words to help Lisa understand.

We began playing a little telepathy game. I'd ask Lisa what she'd had for dinner at school that day. Then she'd write down what she'd been given and I'd write down what I thought she'd eaten and then we'd swap papers. I was always right and Lisa's reading and writing came on a treat.

The only area where things weren't going so well was my love life. Kevin and I were drifting further and further apart. After so many months of ill health, pregnancy and then a major operation I didn't have much energy to spare and what I did have, I directed towards Lisa and Liam.

I suppose I wasn't much fun for Kevin and he began to go out of an evening on his own. I was more than happy for an excuse to go to bed early with a hot drink and a magazine so I didn't mind, but one night as I switched off the lamp, Peter appeared beside me.

'It's not going to last,' he said, and I knew exactly what he was talking about. 'He's with another woman right now.'

And as he spoke I looked at the blank wall at the foot of the bed and a picture of Kevin and a slight, pretty girl with shoulder-length dark hair formed before my eyes.

Some time later I heard Kevin come in and I put my dressing gown on and went to say hello. He looked vaguely sheepish when he saw me and his mouth was unusually red.

'Sorry, did I wake you up?'

'No,' I said calmly, 'I was reading. What's that round your mouth?'

'Nothing,' said Kevin.

'It looks like red lipstick,' I said.

'There's something wrong with you. Of course it's not lipstick,' said Kevin, turning away.

So I went down to the kitchen and came back with a piece of kitchen roll. I handed it to him.

'Wipe your mouth with that then.'

'You're mad, you,' Kevin said, but he dabbed half-heartedly at his lips. The kitchen paper came away from his face, streaked with red.

'Wearing lipstick now are you?' I said, showing him the evidence. 'Don't you know by now it's no good lying to me? I always know. She's petite with shoulder-length dark hair.'

Kevin shrugged and walked away. 'You're talking rubbish,' he said over his shoulder. 'Believe what you want to believe.'

But it wasn't a question of faith or lack of faith: I'd seen the evidence with my own eyes. My mind went back to the time when I was a little girl at home, given a sudden mysterious glimpse of my father flirting with a heavily made-up blonde. And I knew now that she wasn't the last of his illicit girlfriends. Once that sort of thing started it didn't stop. It was very sad but I refused to put up with what Mum had put up with. It only led to more and more unhappiness. I would rather be completely skint and happy with my kids, than living a lie with the wrong man.

If I could have made the relationship work I would have done, but things had deteriorated too far. Now I understood why I'd never been able to see myself as Mrs Davis.

A few days later I was confiding in my friend Liz and I described the girl I'd seen in my mind's eye with Kevin and the place where they were sitting. Now it was Liz's turn to look sheepish. 'My God Di, you're so right. I don't know how to tell you this but I was there that night with some friends and we saw him. That girl looked exactly like you said and they were eating each other. We all saw them together but it was so embarrassing. No-one liked to say anything to you. We didn't know what to do.'

The relationship was over. We staggered on a little while longer but we both knew it had run its course. In the end Kevin moved out to a flat and Lisa, Liam and I were left in the house on our own. Yet it didn't seem right somehow. Despite our failure this was meant to be a house of love. The longer I stayed there without a partner the more I felt that I shouldn't be there. The house ought to be returned to its rightful owners, the young couple who had lavished such care on it.

The more I thought about it the more this idea nagged at me and I knew it was the right thing to do. So

I asked around, got friends to contact friends, and eventually I tracked down the couple who'd had to move.

'Would you like to have the house back?' I asked them.

'We'd love to,' said the husband, 'but unfortunately we couldn't afford it.'

'Well, supposing I rented it to you?' I asked. 'Until you were in a position to buy.'

His eyes widened in amazement. 'Could you do that? That would be perfect.'

'Of course,' I said. 'I could do with something smaller.'

And so the real owners came back and Lisa, Liam and I moved into a smaller place not far away. As we carried the last of our things out to the car, the old lady in the back room gave me a big smile of thanks.

I knew this was the perfect solution.

Chapter Fourteen

The young man showing me round gave me a devastating smile – he was very good looking – and gestured towards the old-fashioned cottage piano that stood against the wall.

'Would you mind if I leave the piano here? Only I haven't got room for it and I can't get rid of it. It's my sister's.'

I glanced at the piano. It made the room look homely and maybe Lisa could learn to play. Even if she didn't, it would be fun for both kids to mess about on.

'That's not a problem,' I said, 'I like it. As long as you don't mind the children having a go.' And as I spoke I rested my hand lightly on the warm polished wood of the piano lid. Instantly the image of a beautiful young woman with glossy chestnut hair shot into my mind. I could see her sitting at this very piano, running smooth fingers up and down the keys.

'God, your sister's glamorous,' I said.

'She's an actress,' said the young man. 'The plant's hers as well.'

'I was just admiring that,' I said, glancing back at the huge, jungly specimen that stood in the corner beside the fireplace. If you tried to buy a plant that size it would cost a fortune. 'It's gorgeous. Are you going to leave that too?'

'If you like,' said the young man.

And that's how I came to be the temporary owner of Catherine Zeta Jones's piano and giant pot plant.

I'd seen the advert for David Jones's neat terraced house in Pwll Street in the evening paper and it seemed exactly what I was looking for. It was far smaller and not as lavishly decorated as our previous home in Clare Street, but the rent was cheap, it was convenient for Mum and Debbie, and it had a happy atmosphere. I felt secure there. What's more, this David Jones seemed an exceptionally nice man. He was moving back to live with his parents and was probably glad of the rent money, but despite this he obviously realised that I was going through a tough time.

'Look, don't worry about the rent this week while you move in,' he said. 'We can sort it all out when you're settled.'

Which was very nice of him. We went on to become great friends. David loved photography, in fact his excellent photographs were all over the house, but he wasn't working as a photographer. A kind-hearted and immensely practical man, he was helping his uncle out in the Skoda garage at the end of the road. He drove around in a big silver van and he looked in once a week to collect the rent. He was so handsome and we got on so well that everyone used to think we must be having an affair, but we weren't. We truly were just good buddies.

As for his sister Catherine, she wasn't yet the big star she was destined to become. She was just a pretty young actress who was making an impression in a popular TV show – *The Darling Buds of May*. There was no hint then of the spectacular future she had in store.

Swansea's a small world and I was fascinated to discover from David that Catherine had been a student at the same dance class my parents had briefly let me attend when I was little. I'd loved dancing, particularly tap, and Mum bought me the shoes with pom-poms and a little skirt. We were a similar age and, who knows, Catherine and I might even have been in the same class. But then my father clamped down ever tighter on Mum's housekeeping money and she couldn't afford to send me any more, so that put paid to any thoughts of a dancing career!

David usually stopped for a cup of tea and a chat when he came to collect the rent and it wasn't long before he got to hear about my psychic abilities. Could I see anything for him he wanted to know? Strictly speaking I'd given up readings, of course. It wasn't easy to get by, but with help from Mum and Kevin, who called in regularly to see Liam, we managed, and I really wanted to prove to myself that I could be a full-time mum and devote myself to the children.

But David was my landlord after all so I made an exception. When I tuned in to David I got a strong impression of America, which surprised me because he seemed so settled in Wales. I could see him in a big, sprawling house in the States and it looked like he owned it.

'David, you're going to be a famous person, and you're going to live in America,' I said. 'In fact you're going to be in films. You're going to be a film producer.'

David laughed. 'Fat chance of that, Diane. Fat chance. I can't see that happening.'

But he was interested. 'D'you really think so though?' he asked after a minute or two. 'I'd love to be a producer. It's what I've always wanted to do.'

'Well, it's going to happen,' I said, 'and you'll be well known in America.'

David shook his head. 'No, I'd never move from Wales.'

Yet as the years went on that's exactly what he did. He went into film production – now runs his own company I believe – and spends most of his time in his lovely home in the USA.

'What about Catherine?' asked David. 'She loves all this sort of thing. Can you see anything for her? Is she going to do well too?'

'To find out about Catherine all I need to do is sit by the fire and put my hand in the plant pot!' I joked, nodding at the huge leaves that were spreading ever further across the alcove. But then I concentrated and tried to push my mind into Catherine's future. I got an impression of success so great it made me gasp.

'She's going to do fantastically well,' I told David. 'She's going to be a big star. There are problems with a relationship at the moment, but she mustn't worry because she's not meant to be with him.'

David was amazed and impressed.

I looked harder and I saw Catherine with an older man, an actor. His face was familiar but I couldn't put a name to it. Still, Catherine seemed very happy. She was smiling up at him, full of joy.

'I think she's going to be with an older man,' I went on. 'He's an actor too and he's the son of a famous actor. I see her with two little boys. She's going to be very, very famous but she'll never forget where she came from. She'll keep close links with Wales.'

'I can't wait to tell her,' said David. 'She'll be fascinated.'

Oddly enough, one day a few months later I was polishing the piano when a picture of Catherine suddenly leapt into my mind. She was walking on a beautiful, pale sand beach somewhere hot and sunny. She was dressed in flowing white and she was strolling hand in hand with an older American film star.

It looked exactly like a wedding scene and I assumed that she was going to make a film with a film star in which she played his screen bride. It never occurred to me that I might have been looking at real life!

Years later, of course, as the whole world knows, Catherine did become a big star and marry Michael Douglas. So far they have two children, a girl and a boy, but I reckon there's another little boy still to come. We'll have to wait and see.

David continued to be very kind over the rent but my finances were in a poor state and it was often a struggle to pay the bills. I still wanted to be a 100 per cent mum so I tried to be as creative as possible with what cash I had.

Kevin and I had parted not long before Lisa's tenth birthday and after I'd ordered a cake for her. It was too late to cancel it, but I really didn't know where the money to pay for it was going to come from. I prayed very hard for several nights and asked the Lined Man for help, but no extra cash fell through the letter box. I was still fretting the day I was to pick it up when the baker's rang.

'We're terribly sorry,' they said. 'There's been a mistake. You ordered a cake for a tenth birthday and it's come back with the number nine on it. I know it's not what you want, but if you'd still like to take it, you can have it on us.'

It was the answer to my prayers. A free cake! Yet although I was very pleased, I was a little concerned too. Lisa was old enough to know the difference between a figure nine and a ten and it would take the edge off her delight if it looked as if she'd been given another little girl's cake.

Then I had an idea. I carefully scraped off the entire number, dug out an old bag of icing sugar from the cupboard, squirted some pink colouring into it and made my own iced one and nought right across the middle of the cake. I'd never done any proper icing before so I wasn't confident, but it came out surprisingly well. Lisa never knew that it hadn't come straight from the baker's like that.

As for me, I enjoyed the experiment so much that I began icing everything in sight. Soon I was honing my skills on fun food for the kids. I piped curly potato hair round cauliflower eyes and smiling carrot mouths on their plates so that happy faces looked back at them when they ate. Or I added pink colouring to the mash and created big grinning potato lips embellished with green pea teeth. It was cheaper than the children's food in the freezer shops and probably healthier too.

Yet even though life was sometimes a struggle for me, I could see that it was far worse for some other unfortunate people. At the top of the hill lived an old lady who could hardly walk. Often when I was out and about with Lisa and Liam in his pushchair, I'd see her tottering along the street pushing her Zimmer frame. She'd recently lost her husband and she didn't know what to do without him. She looked droopy and sad and disoriented.

One day as I walked past her house on my way to take Lisa to school I saw the old lady at her front door talking to the milkman. She was standing unsteadily on the black and white tiles, leaning on her walking frame, and the milkman seemed to be badgering her.

'You've gotta pay, love,' I heard him saying. 'You can't just have milk and not pay the bill. You're gonna have to hand over the money.'

Confused, the old woman produced a battered purse from her apron pocket. She fumbled to open it without letting go of her walking frame but her arthritic fingers weren't dexterous enough to manage. The purse spun out of her hands and fell to the ground, spilling its contents – no more than a few coppers – across the milkman's feet.

He picked them up and gave them back to her and she started to try to count the coins, although it was quite clear that however much she owed, they wouldn't be enough. My throat constricted in pity for her. I glanced down at Lisa who was tugging my hand because I'd slowed down so much, and when I looked back I saw an old man had come to stand behind the old lady and tears were running down his face. There was something about the slight fuzziness to his outline that told me he was a spirit man, only recently passed over.

'She can't see the money. She can't find her glasses,' he said to me with a look as if his heart was breaking.

I glared at the milkman in anger. Leave her alone! I thought, can't you see she hasn't got it? The milkman seemed to pick up my thoughts.

'Tell you what – I'll come back tomorrow,' he said impatiently. 'Give you time to count it out.'

And as he walked back to his milk float I heard him mutter, 'She won't be on my milk list much longer.'

I was furious and I felt like going and tackling him there and then, but Lisa was late for school and starting to fret so I had to hurry away. The incident played on my mind, though, and for more than one reason. I knew I had to help the old lady, that was obvious, but there was something else too. I had a strong feeling that I'd seen the old man for a purpose; it was as if I was being reminded that there was still work to do. Everywhere I looked there were people who needed help and it was about time I got back to it.

That night I searched through all my bags and pockets and even down the back of the sofa for any spare cash I could find. I managed to scrape together about twenty pounds. Then I put it in an envelope, wrote MILKMAN in big letters on the front and, when darkness fell, I slipped out and posted it through the old lady's door.

Milk bottles continued to appear on her step so I assumed that she'd managed to pay the bill, but it wasn't many weeks after that that a For Sale board went up outside the house. The old lady had died, as desperate to be reunited with her husband, I'm sure, as he was to be with her.

I often thought about the incident after that and one night, just as I was falling asleep, Peter appeared.

'Come on, I want to show you something,' he said, and the next thing I knew he was taking me flying again.

We floated away from Swansea – but not very far away this time, only out into the countryside – and I found myself looking down onto a small village clustered round a crossroads. Just outside the village, high on a hill was a beautiful, wild area with a silvery lake fringed by rushes and a white tower reflected in the water.

'That's where you're going,' said Peter.

It made no sense at all. There was hardly anything there. Why on earth would I go to the middle of nowhere? Then we moved on and I saw the big red-brick house he'd pointed out to me years before. This time I took in a bay window and some white columns at the front. But before I could ask too many questions I was falling asleep again.

'Follow your dream,' I thought I heard Peter say as he faded away.

When I thought about it the next morning, I realised with irritation that I'd managed to crash out yet again just as I was about to discover something important. I couldn't help wondering why these sessions always turned into such riddles. Why couldn't Peter just tell me plainly what he wanted me to know? Why did I always have to work out his meaning for myself?

From far away I thought I heard Peter's rueful laugh. 'Isn't that the whole point? You're catching on.'

Sometimes he made my brain ache, he really did.

Yet there was change in the air. A hairdresser friend of mine, Lynne, lived nearby and she often popped in for a chat. She'd trim my hair for me and I'd give her a quick reading. Lynne was convinced that I needed to get out more, and whenever I could get Mum to babysit she invited me out with her and her boyfriend Paul. One night the three of us were having a quiet drink in a pub in town when a friend of Paul's walked in. He was a very attractive man, slim and smart in a well-cut three-piece suit and I liked him instantly. His name was Peter Lazarus and he was a solicitor. For some reason a prediction from one of my fellow students at Jeff Marsh's Rugged Cross meetings came wafting back to me down the years. 'You're going to marry a pro-fessional man, a man who wears a suit every day,' she'd said.

I pushed the stupid thought away, but all the same there was an instant attraction between us. From then on I seemed to bump into Peter all the time. Once again I wasn't looking for a relationship and neither was he. He was in the process of splitting up from his wife and he intended to move into his grandmother's old bungalow in the village of Cross Hands, a few miles outside Swansea. Neither of us wanted any more com-plications in our lives and yet the chemistry between us was so strong we couldn't ignore it.

Peter took to phoning me regularly. We'd talk through my problems for ages and then we'd talk through his. At one point he phoned me from holiday in Corfu in a terrible state.

'Hello Peter,' I said in surprise when I picked up the phone, 'I thought you were playing cricket in Corfu.'

'I am,' said Peter, 'but I've just done something a bit rash. I've resigned!'

Peter had long been getting fed up with the way the office was run at work, but when he'd phoned from Corfu to check the progress made on the cases he'd left behind and discovered there was practically none, it was the last straw for him.

'I told them what I thought of them,' he said. 'It seemed like a good idea at the time but now . . . I'm thinking about the mortgage and the car and . . . d'you think I should fly back?'

I tuned in for him over the phone wire and instantly reassuring pictures began to form.

'It's okay, Peter. You might as well stay where you are and enjoy yourself. You're going to be fine. You're going to have your own practice.'

'I can't see that happening,' said Peter. 'What am I going to do? There's the divorce and maintenance and the house . . . How can I cope?'

I put on my coolest, calmest voice. 'Peter, you're going to be fine. It'll work out for you. Don't worry. Stop panicking. You *are* going to have your own practice. What's more it's going to be at the end of a row of shops and there's some sort of connection with a butcher's.'

Yet even now I didn't trust my gift 100 per cent and I was silently keeping my fingers crossed. 'Oh my God,' I thought to myself, 'I hope that comes true.'

I needn't have worried. Peter came home, sorted things out and began looking for premises in Cross Hands. He was actually offered one property and seemed quite certain it would be perfect for him.

'What d'you think, Diane?' he asked me. 'Is this the right place?'

'No, I don't think it is,' I said.

Peter was quite cross. 'Look, Diane, I've had a survey done and everything and it's ideal.'

'Well, I'm sorry,' I said, 'but you did ask and I can't see it happening.'

He went off in a bit of a strop about that. He got in a really bad mood with me, and I wasn't pleased either. I mean, if you ask, you need to be prepared to take the answer, don't you?

Anyway, shortly afterwards the sale fell through but, before he could get too despondent, Peter was offered another place – a former butcher's shop at the end of the terrace. There was even plenty of space for parking out the back, which there hadn't been at the first property, and everything fell into place, just as I'd predicted it would.

Despite the odd minor squabble – probably caused by the stress of our precarious lives – Peter and I became great friends and then more than friends. I seemed to spend half my life in the car driving backwards and forwards to Cross Hands and in the end the most sensible thing was to move in together.

I hesitated for a while over whether it was the right thing to do. It meant uprooting the children, moving to a different area further away from my friends and family, and after two failed relationships I was nervous about making another mistake. Yet events seemed to conspire to drive me out of the house in Pwll Street that had been my sanctuary for so long.

Once again, though I'd kept a low profile, people had started discovering where I lived and began to knock on the door at all hours of the day and night. Often they were so desperate I'd have to chase Lisa and Liam up to the bedroom so that I could let them in to discuss their troubles, but it wasn't very fair to the children.

Then one night I woke suddenly to find the Lined Man in the room. He pointed down the stairs and I had the sudden certainty that there was someone there.

Quietly I reached for the phone at my bedside and called Peter's number.

'Peter!' I whispered. 'Sorry to wake you but I think there's someone downstairs – or at least outside.'

'I'll be right over,' he said. 'I'll call the police.'

I put the phone down but I couldn't just sit there and wait. My babies were asleep in the next room and I had to protect them. I crept silently down the stairs. There was no-one there, but as I tiptoed into the kitchen I saw through the glass of the door the figure of a teenage boy, a dark hood pulled up over his head and a crowbar in his hand.

I let out what was a mighty cross between a yell and a scream – so loud it startled even me. The boy jumped a mile, stared through the glass for a second but obviously couldn't make out who was there, then turned round and ran.

By the time the police arrived there was no sign of him.

'So how did you know there was an intruder outside?' asked the young constable later, notebook and pencil poised. 'Did you hear a noise? Footsteps? He knocked against the bin perhaps?'

'No, nothing,' I said. 'I didn't hear anything. I just felt it.'

The policeman gave me a wary look. 'A noise must have woken you. You just don't remember.'

They never did catch the boy but I often wondered what would have happened if I hadn't woken up. Would he have broken open the door and got in? Supposing I'd gone downstairs then? It made me shiver to think of it.

My sense of vulnerability, added to the feeling of being at everyone's beck and call, was causing strain to build up inside me and maybe this made my psychic defences weaken. I don't know but, whatever the reason, I had another even more terrifying encounter not long afterwards. This time there was no point in calling the police because it was no human intruder that disturbed the night.

I woke suddenly in the dark to hear sinister footsteps climbing the stairs towards my bedroom. Yet without even moving a muscle I knew this was no burglar coming to steal from me. What was out there made no effort to creep. The footfalls were heavy, regular and undisguised. Something evil was heading slowly towards my room. The air turned cold as ice and little tendrils of pure horror were seeping under the door. I could feel an immense power out there, a power far too strong for me. I'd never known anything like it. This man, for even though I couldn't see him I could tell that once it had been a man, was a thoroughly bad person. The worst I'd ever come across.

'Go away! Go away!' I ordered, sending out all the negative energy I could summon, but it bounced off him like a child's tiny rubber-tipped toy arrow. He kept on coming.

'Go away!' I said again. But sheer terror flooded the room. He had stepped inside. I could feel him standing there, enormous and black, at the foot of the bed. I was too petrified even to scream. I dived under the covers and pulled them over my head.

'I'm okay,' I told myself. 'He can't hurt me. I'm on earth and he's not. He can't do anything physical to me. I'm fine. I'm fine. He can't hurt me.'

But my fingers were trembling with fear and I didn't believe the words I was saying. Why I didn't shout for the Lined Man I don't know; instead I found myself reciting the Lord's Prayer. Over and over. 'Our Father who art in Heaven . . . Our Father who art in Heaven . . .'

And gradually the darkness lessened, the temperature began to rise and finally the presence faded away. I lay there shaking for a long time after that, until dawn brightened the room and made everything normal again. I hadn't even stepped out of bed and yet I was as exhausted as if I'd been seven rounds with a prize fighter.

The time had come to move on, I realised. I didn't want to agree to live with Peter for the wrong reasons but I knew that I wasn't doing that. I'd found true love at last and it was inevitable that we would be together; it was just the timing of our setting up home that had been in doubt. Now I knew that I was ready to leave Pwll Street for the green open spaces of Cross Hands.

Chapter Fifteen

It was a bright spring morning but the wind was whipping in from the coast, shredding the little white clouds overhead and whooshing down the high street in spirited gusts.

'Uh oh,' I thought, noticing the way the bushes out the back were tossing, 'I'll just . . .'

Too late. There was a crash from outside and the large, beaming Welsh lady with the pointy hat and big white apron fell flat on her face again, pearly smile crushed against the paving stones. I went out and stood her up for the umpteenth time. She was swung back, painted face barely scratched, cheerful expression undimmed.

'I suppose you think that's funny?' I told her affectionately, but in fact I couldn't be happier. I stared up at the smart cream and black sign over the shop front: Sweet Memories. I still couldn't resist going out to look at it whenever I could find an excuse. It was perfect and I could hardly believe it was actually mine. I'd done it at last. I had my own little tearoom. My dream had come true.

The anxious days in Pwll Street seemed years rather

than just a few months away. Peter and I had set up home in a lovely old farmhouse hidden away down a winding road in the back of beyond not far from Cross Hands. And to my amazement I recognised it as the village I'd seen on my trips with my cousin Peter all those months ago. The farmhouse had low beams and flagstone floors and a traditional kitchen with a big wooden table in the middle. It was rented out partly furnished, which was ideal because neither Peter nor I had much furniture. Best of all it was so tucked away that unless they were invited, no-one would ever be able to find me.

We all settled happily into the farm and Peter was also getting his new practice off the ground. But it got me thinking. If Peter could start his own business, maybe I could too. 'Follow your dream,' cousin Peter had advised me that time he showed me Cross Hands, long before I'd even heard of the place. I hadn't known what he'd meant then, but I did recall that the only dream I'd ever really had was to open my own little bistro or tearoom. The idea seemed as out of reach as the moon when I was living in Pwll Street but now, quite unexpectedly, it appeared to be coming within my grasp.

The couple who'd moved into the house I shared with Kevin in Clare Street were finally in a position to buy it and once the mortgage was paid off, I was left for the first time with a little money in the bank. Unfortunately it wasn't enough to start a tearoom.

Yet I had this vision of how my tearoom should be. I

could see it clearly. There was a big old Welsh dresser and flowers on the tables, and proper waitresses in black uniforms and white aprons zipping backwards and forwards with plates of freshly baked scones.

'Well, why don't you do what everyone else does to start a business?' said Peter. 'Why don't you get a bank loan?'

A bank loan? It seemed a frightening prospect but Peter encouraged me. He brought me some forms and I drew up plans of what I intended to do, went to see the bank manager and, to my amazement, I was given a loan.

I found a converted house to rent in the main street in Cross Hands, just across the road from Peter's solicitors' practice, and set about decorating it and furnishing it. The position was excellent, being right on the main road, and the building even had rooms upstairs where I could give psychic readings and healing. There was no longer any need for people to come to my home for help, and with luck this would mean I could keep my work and my family life separate. Which had to be good news for our relationship.

I had great fun scouring car boot sales, junk shops, auction rooms and house clearances to deck out my tearoom. I picked up a huge mirror for £10 and a load of chairs from an old church, a stack of willow-pattern plates from a car boot sale and a pile of tables from a defunct nightclub. A friend's husband made my delight-ful but over-skittish Welsh lady, complete with painted menu at the side. The most expensive thing was the traditional dresser which I had specially built to fit by an elderly local craftsman.

I lost about a stone in weight and all my nails as I worked round the clock, cleaning, sandpapering and painting. One of the final touches was the name; although this was so important, I couldn't think what to call my tearoom. I asked everyone I knew for suggestions, but nothing seemed quite right until I was chatting to my friend Sue who was helping me. Her mother had recently passed over and apparently she'd been very good at neat turns of phrase and slogans. I wondered if she might be able to assist from the spirit world.

'Why not ask her?' said Sue.

So I concentrated on Sue, silently asking her mother to come close, and as I felt a loving presence envelop Sue, I asked what I should call the tearoom. 'Sweet Memories' came a soft pretty voice in my ear.

It seemed absolutely perfect. Sweet Memories the tearoom became.

I was like a child at Christmas. I hired some uniformed waitresses, busied myself in the kitchen baking scones and cakes, and now and again I went up to my therapy rooms upstairs to do a reading or some healing.

Cross Hands was a much smaller place then than it is now and it was still very traditionally Welsh. I feared that some of the older people might disapprove of my work, and I think that for a while they expected me to be walking around with two devil horns, but as time passed they got used to me and even one of the elders of the chapel came for a reading.

Baking was bliss and I was very happy in the kitchen in my big apron with a heap of flour. Yet it wasn't long before the Lined Man and cousin Peter started dropping in more frequently when I was on the edge of sleep. When I woke I couldn't remember what they'd been saying, but my instincts told me that I was moving forward again.

One day I was suddenly seized with the idea that the menus could do with smartening up. They were getting a bit battered and dog-eared and I felt it was time to invest in something more professional looking. I found a small printer in the phone book which seemed just the kind of place that could help and I drove over with a few sketches to Llanelli where they were based to see what they could do. But when I got there it seemed I'd chosen the wrong moment.

'I'm sorry,' said the man who came out of the office to help. 'It's my son who does the printing and he's not here at the moment.'

He was an easy-going man, very polite, with wavy grey hair and a neat little goatee beard, and he was so friendly I thought I might as well tell him what I had in mind anyway.

He listened carefully and glanced at my sketches with what seemed to be a professional eye. 'But you know, you could do this yourself,' he said in his posh English voice. 'You could easily run off what you want, keep the document on your computer, and then change it whenever you need and run off a few more.'

That's odd, I thought to myself, he's talking himself out of a bit of business.

'Whereabouts are you anyway?' he asked.

'Out at Cross Hands,' I said. 'We haven't been open very long. It's a tearoom with therapy rooms upstairs.'

'Therapy rooms?'

'Well, I'm a psychic and I do readings,' I explained reluctantly.

To my surprise the man leaned forward eagerly.

'Really?' he said. 'That's fascinating. I'm looking for a medium right now. I'm a crime writer. I write books about murders and mysteries. I've written about Jack the Ripper and various unsolved crimes, and I've been thinking about asking a medium to see if they can pick up anything on the cases I'm investigating now. Have you ever done any work on crimes?'

'No,' I said.

'Well, would you like to?' he asked.

I never could resist a challenge and I heard myself say cautiously, 'I wouldn't mind.'

'Okay,' he said. 'Well, give me your number and I'll sort out a challenge for you! I'd like to take you to the scene of a murder and see if you can pick anything up.'

'Okay,' I heard myself say.

And that's how I met criminologist Bob Hinton.

It wasn't long before he called me.

'You're in the Cross Hands tearooms aren't you?' he said. 'Meet me in the pub car park down the road and we'll go from there. I've got your challenge.'

I began to feel a bit nervous and wondered why I'd let

myself in for such a stunt. I'd never quite understood this 'see what you can pick up' about a place idea because it seemed to me that you needed a link between people, not bricks and mortar. Why should someone connected with a building from long ago want to talk to me, or Bob for that matter, when they didn't know us? From the sort of work Bob said he did, it sounded as if all the people connected to his murders would be long gone. Still, I'd promised. 'Okay,' I said to the Lined Man and to cousin Peter. 'You'd better help me!'

As I swung into the car park, Bob's car pulled along-side mine. He jumped out and came striding over. He was dressed in cream trousers and a safari-type jacket with little pockets all round it, full of the tools of his trade: dictaphone, notebook and various pens.

'Okay, Bob,' I said. 'Where're we going?'

Bob grinned. 'We're here! We're going inside.'

And he gestured towards the pub.

'Here?' I glanced at the pub dubiously. It looked quite nice from the outside and I'd not been into it yet, but I thought I recalled someone telling me it was a bit on the rough side.

'Yep,' said Bob, 'they're expecting us.'

So in we went and whoever had told me it was a bit rough must have been thinking of somewhere else because it couldn't have been friendlier. At that time of day the bars were deserted but Jan, the bubbly landlady, met us and showed us into the lounge.

'Would you like a drink?' she asked.

And I accepted a glass of water because I'd discovered

that the more water I drink before working, the better the results seem to be. It's almost as if I need to detox before I get started.

'Okay,' said Bob. 'Why don't you see if you can pick anything up upstairs.'

We walked out into the hall and as I looked towards the stairs a woman appeared. She was a little dishevelled, quite hot and sweaty and you didn't need to be psychic to realise she was drunk. She staggered slightly as she negotiated the steps and I could smell alcohol on her breath. I began to feel dizzy and my head spun, just as hers must have done.

She turned and looked at me. 'I'm Mary,' she said and she showed me her hands. They were worn and crooked. She wanted me to know that she was a hard worker.

'Come on,' she said, when she was certain I understood. 'Come with me. I want to show you what happened.'

'Oh yes, someone died here,' I said to Bob who was watching me curiously, 'someone was killed here.' And I started to follow Mary.

As I walked the years fell away and I was back in the 1920s. The fitted carpet on the staircase seemed to fade into the background and through it I could see plain wooden steps.

'It's August 30 1920,' Mary said and she led me onto the landing where corridors went in all directions in the shape of a letter H. I could see eleven doors stretching away at intervals but Mary marched straight towards one of them.

'Not that one,' she said, dismissing one of the other doors with a wave of her crooked hand. 'That's the bathroom. I cracked my head on the beam this morning. I've still got the bump. It hurt. It really hurt. Now – this is it.'

And she led me into the room that in the present day belonged to Jan's son. Instantly a cold blast hit my face and I knew that this was the room where Mary had been killed. I saw not the normal boy paraphernalia but an old-fashioned carpet, threadbare grey with a large, faded red flower just off-centre.

'This isn't my room, it's the maid's room,' said Mary. 'I'll show you my room.'

And a picture flashed into my head of a larger, sleeker room with old-fashioned furniture and a heavy, mahogany dressing table with silver-backed brushes, cut-glass scent bottles and little crocheted mats arranged artistically across the top.

'I'd had a bit to drink,' Mary said, 'so I came in here to lie down,' and we were back in the maid's bedroom again.

And then I had a sudden vision of her husband. A stern man, quite polite and outwardly kind and generous, but behind closed doors a violent and nasty personality.

'He used to slap me across the face with the back of his hand,' said Mary. 'It was over the milk you know. All over the milk.'

Then I glanced at the bed again and was horrified to see that Mary was now lying on it, quite dead. One hand was draped on the floor, the other was on the counterpane, there was bruising all over her chest and neck, her eyes were wide open and her tongue was hanging out. I gasped in shock and started to cry, but Mary made me carry on watching. There was a flash and I saw her husband – one knee on her chest, hands clamped around her neck, viciously strangling her as she struggled.

Then the husband was gone. Mary was lying lifeless on top of the bed and the maid came in and screamed. At this point Mary was still breathing but her brain had gone. She'd been starved of oxygen.

'My mother's here. What's my mother doing here?' Mary asked.

I couldn't tell her but I'd seen enough. I felt clammy and ill and my throat hurt. I wanted to get out of there. It was like watching the most disturbing film and being unable to leave the cinema. I turned to Bob who was still recording everything I said.

'I've got to go now Bob,' I said breathlessly. 'I've got to fetch Liam from school.'

'Oh, of course. Of course,' said Bob.

He'd given nothing away. I had no idea whether what I'd said tallied with what he was expecting, or even if this was the case he'd intended me to investigate.

'Not much is known about this murder today,' he said, as I was leaving. 'I'm going to have to do a lot more digging and checking of the old records to find out what happened.'

'Fine,' I said. It didn't matter much what the records said. I knew Mary was glad just to have been able to put her side of the story.

A few weeks later, Bob rang to tell me he was astonished at what he'd discovered and also at the accuracy of my impressions. He'd spent a considerable amount of time getting hold of old court records and autopsy reports from 1920 and found that Mary had indeed suffered extensive bruising to her chest and neck because her killer had knelt on her chest while strangling her. She had been discovered lying in exactly the position I described, she was found in the maid's bedroom not her own, and she even had a bump on her head from the low beam.

Witness statements described how Mary Jenkins and her husband Griffith, who was somewhat older than Mary, did not get on too well. Large bruises had previously been seen on Mary's face where her husband hit her, and some months before her death purple marks were noticed around her neck, once again inflicted by her husband. On August 30 1920 Mary had hit her head on a low beam in the bathroom. She and her husband had also quarrelled about the 'separation of the milk'. Griffith had bought a 'milk separator' and was annoyed that neither his wife nor the maid had used it that day. We weren't sure what this machine was used for, something to do with skimming off the milk fat to make cream perhaps? But whatever Griffith wanted done with the milk, the failure to carry out his instructions caused a fierce argument.

Later Mary retired upstairs for a rest and refused to come down when her husband sent for her. Later still she was found dead on the maid's bed.

What's more, an old newspaper story had recorded the distressing news that Mary's mother, who lived nearby, had been woken in the night and told that Mary was 'ill'. The poor woman came rushing down to the hotel to look after her daughter, only to discover that she'd been murdered.

Eventually Griffith Jenkins was found guilty of manslaughter and sentenced to five years. I reckon Mary was aggrieved that he had got off so lightly, and I must say I can see her point. Maybe that was why she was so keen to tell me her story.

As Bob unravelled the whole sorry case, I think I was almost as amazed as he was at the accuracy of my information. I didn't doubt what Mary had said to me but I still couldn't quite believe what happened. How had I been able to see the whole dreadful event replayed as if I was watching a film? It was almost as uncanny to me as it was to Bob. I had no idea how I did it, or why I could do it. It just happened. It was fascinating but unnerving too, and I can't say it was pleasant to have to watch such dreadful things, even if they had occurred more than eighty years before.

'I don't know how you did it,' said Bob, as if reading my mind, 'but with the short notice I gave you, if you managed to research all that in advance, you're in the wrong job. You'd make a fortune as a researcher. It took me weeks to discover what you told me in half an hour.'

I was flattered. 'Well, I'm glad you're pleased.'

'We'll have to do this again,' he added enthusiastically.

'Okay,' I heard myself saying once more. Why did I keep *saying* that? What was the *matter* with me?

A little while later I got another call from Bob, asking if I'd go up to London with him and a reporter and photographer from a Welsh newspaper to see if we could come up with any new information on the Jill Dando murder. The whole country was still baffled and upset by the loss of TV presenter Jill, who was such a popular and inoffensive person. They wanted me to see if I could gather any psychic impressions that might help the police track down the killer, and they hoped that Bob would be able to view the scene from a criminologist's angle and come up with some fresh theories.

I wasn't sure that I could help but I was glad to have a try. Whenever I'd seen Jill on TV she had struck me as such a nice, genuine person.

In the car on the way to Jill's London home I glanced down and suddenly saw a pair of shapely legs in glossy, high-sheen tights with patent leather stiletto-heeled shoes. Sadly they weren't my legs, I was definitely not wearing high-sheen tights that day; I was warmly wrapped in black trousers and a beige coat. Then I got an impression of a smart pencil skirt and blouse and finally there was Jill's bright face, smiling at me. She was beautiful, and with her short blonde hair and big blue eyes she put me in mind of Princess Diana.

The journey up the motorway was long and tedious, but when we finally arrived at the pretty, white terraced house in the leafy street where Jill had lived, Bob was surprised that it was so unpretentious. The newspapers had described Jill's home as being worth close to a million pounds and he was expecting something far grander.

'That's London for you,' said the reporter.

Bob suggested that we split up into two parties to gather our impressions and then meet up afterwards in the pub, so that's what we did. I went with the reporter and Bob with the photographer.

I stood across the road and focused on the house and as I did so Jill came back and hovered behind me. I felt as if she was regarding her old home too.

'He'd been watching me,' she said, 'for quite a while. I knew him. I'd seen his face.'

I got the impression she'd been quite jittery about it. She had the feeling something wasn't quite right, but who would ever have expected that something so dreadful could happen? It wasn't as if she was a politician or anyone controversial. Probably the worst she could imagine was a burglary or some sort of sex attack.

'He's got a flat near here,' Jill said, 'and there's lots of newspapers in it. *Lots* of newspapers. And he's been into the shop just down there and bought cigarettes. Regularly.'

Then I got a swift vision of a man walking calmly away after the murder, only to return later to his flat and stash the weapon.

All this was before police finally arrested Barry George, the man who was eventually convicted of the murder. But after my visit a little white tent appeared outside the house again and police activity resumed. Whether it had any connection with what I said I've no idea.

When Barry George was caught, he certainly seemed to fit my description of the killer, and yet I'm still not quite convinced it was him. Neither's Bob. Bob was quite sure that this case had all the hallmarks of a contract killing and that the murder was carried out by a hired assassin – hired by someone who knew Jill. Only time will tell, but I'm sure the whole truth will come out one of these days.

Back at the tearoom life went on in a more down to earth fashion. One day I looked out at the customers sitting chatting, sipping tea and nibbling cakes and noticed a gentleman who seemed vaguely out of place. He was alone in the corner and as I stared at him I saw quite clearly the word 'TAXMAN' written in the air over his head. It looked so funny I had to suppress a smile.

I sauntered over. 'Hello,' I said, 'I haven't seen you around here before.'

He looked a little alarmed that I'd noticed him. 'Have you not? Well I'm a local. I'm from Talfenny.'

'That's nice.' I said, 'And what do you do in Talfenny?'

'I'm a financial adviser, a qualified financial adviser.'

'Really,' I said, 'well it's strange I don't know you. It's always good to have financial advice.'

He looked even more uncomfortable so I decided to stop teasing him. I wandered back to the kitchen. 'That's the taxman,' I said to the girls.

Sure enough, a few weeks later I had a letter from the tax office asking me to pay them a visit. But fortunately my books were in good order and there was no problem.

'I know you sent an inspector down,' I said.

'Oh, I don't suppose that was us,' said the tax woman, lowering her eyes and shuffling some papers about her desk. 'I don't know anything about that.'

But I did. 'It was a tax inspector plain as plain,' I said. She shrugged. Oh well, what did it matter anyway.

'I hope he enjoyed his tea,' I said as I left.

Yet for all the fun with the taxman I was actually spending less and less time in the tearoom these days as my psychic workload began to increase. All sorts of people came to see me and I was surprisingly popular with businessmen. I'd always thought of business people as hard-headed sceptical types, but it was amazing how many of them were more than willing to listen to a bit of supernatural advice about their various projects. One of them was a businessman called Tony Grant, who often popped in for a cup of tea.

'What d'you see for me then?' he asked in his direct way.

'I see property, lots of property,' I said. Then I added, 'If I had money I'd buy property in Cross Hands because this is the place to be. It's going to get much bigger.'

He obviously took me at my word because he went off buying so much property I started nicknaming him the Monopoly Man. He's doing very well these days and sure enough Cross Hands has expanded greatly with a brand new quadrant built at one end full of shops.

Unfortunately not all my businessmen enjoyed such a happy outcome. Clive Fletcher turned up one day in his white BMW, a smart, athletic young man accutomed to success. He wanted to know what he should sell, what he should buy and where he should concentrate next, but I wanted to talk about his health.

'You've got a bad chest,' I told him.

'Yeah, I've had a bug,' said Clive, eager to get back to his business interests.

'You will go to the doctor's about that chest?' I said.

'I've been. It's just an infection,' said Clive.

But I still wasn't happy. 'Promise me you'll go back to the doctor's and get an X-ray done. Ring me and let me know what they say.'

'Yeah, yeah. Don't worry,' said Clive.

And he looked in perfect health, if a little stressed. Yet whenever I glanced at his chest I could see darkness there and I didn't like the look of it.

Clive returned to me several times for more advice on his business and every time I saw him I nagged him about his chest. He was still having problems with it. The 'infection' had not cleared up properly.

I didn't want to say what I thought it was but I urged him with all my might to keep going back to the doctor. Yet each time he did he was told there was nothing to worry about. Finally, eighteen months after my first warning he phoned me.

'Diane, you're never going to believe this,' said Clive,

'the consultant's just told me I've got cancer and it's inoperable. I said to him: "A bloody fortune teller told me about this 18 months ago. If you'd found it then would it have made a difference?" and he said that yes they would probably have been able to cure it then but now it is too late.'

And Clive started to cry and so did I. What could I say?

'And, Di, I've just bought my girlfriend's children a donkey to play with when they come over,' he said, his voice breaking. 'What am I going to do with it now?'

'Oh for goodness sake don't worry about the donkey, Clive,' I said. 'I can help you out there. We live on an old farm. There's stables. We can take care of the donkey for you.'

Sadly Clive passed away a few months later and Daisy, a retired beach donkey who came with her companion, Fluffy the goat, moved in with us and settled down happily in the field behind the house.

Chapter Sixteen

The odd thing was, I didn't know. When my father died I didn't dream any strange dreams, I didn't wake up in the night and see his face, I didn't hear his voice. I didn't even get a visit from the Lined Man or cousin Peter. And my mirrors remained clear and sparkling.

Yet one autumn day in 1997 I popped round to see Mum, the way I always do, and for some reason my hand hesitated just a fraction as I reached for the bell. But that was all.

'Hello love,' said Mum as I walked in. 'I've just put the phone down from talking to your brother. There's bad news . . .'

My heart stopped for an instant – then: 'Your father's died.'

And I started breathing again. How awful of me I thought. Fancy thinking: thank goodness it's only my father! But I did.

'What happened?' I asked, shocked, even though I knew that he couldn't have been in the best of health. Not after losing his leg and drinking even more than he had in my childhood.

'Liver failure, apparently,' said Mum, 'but he hadn't

been well for a long time. What with his leg, and he'd got gout too. He was only 56.'

I looked at Mum closely. She didn't seem upset but I had a sneaking suspicion that deep down a little bit of her still loved him.

'Did he take it badly?' I asked instead, because I knew that despite the ill treatment he'd suffered as a boy, my brother had always been the one who was prepared to forgive our father. He still longed to have the dad he deserved – the dad he should have had all those years ago.

'He seemed okay,' said Mum, 'but I think he was shaken. He's going to the funeral anyway.'

'What about you, Mum? Are you going to the funeral?' I asked.

'Not me,' said Mum, turning away quickly. 'What would I want to go for? I've got no feelings left for him. And that other woman'll be there of course.'

I couldn't blame her. But how did I feel, I asked myself? Had I got any feelings left for him? My eyes were dry and tears refused to well. Where there should have been emotion I could only detect a blank space. Were there really no feelings, or had I just gone numb?

'I expect you'll go though, won't you?' Mum was saying.

'What?'

'To the funeral,' said Mum. 'He was your father after all.'

I sighed. She was doing it again. It was the visiting my father in hospital situation all over again. But then, of course, she was right. He was my father after all. Even though I didn't love him, I should be there.

The thought of having to meet his new family as well, though, was more than I could bear; particularly when I recalled the hostile reception I'd received from Magda all those years ago. I had no reason to expect her to like me any better now than she did then.

'Well, maybe they won't recognise you,' said Peter when I told him about it afterwards. 'Why don't you hide under a big hat? People wear hats to funerals. That way they probably won't even see you.'

It was a brilliant idea so I went out and bought the biggest black hat I could find.

The funeral was held at a bleak, red-brick church in a dingy corner of Cardiff. It was a dreary day and only a handful of mourners had gathered under the dripping trees. Peter and I hung about at the back, me pulling my big hat down over my eyes.

The coffin arrived and was carried slowly across the churchyard and as I watched I found I was looking at my father's hands, but swollen now and twisted. And then my gaze was directed up from the hands to take in the sight of my father, full length, walking beside the pall bearers. I gasped. How changed he was! He seemed shrunken and old, his skin was yellow and there was this terrible, lost look on his face.

Worst of all was what I did not see. When Peter or the Lined Man came to me their figures were always bathed in light and they appeared positively glowing with good health. Yet there was no light around Dad. Quite the reverse. His figure seemed to be trying in vain to pull light towards it out of the surrounding air. He looked gaunt and miserable.

Over the years I'd heard all that old hippy and new-age talk of Karma and I often wondered about it. Until that moment I wasn't sure if I believed in it or not, but now I realised that without a doubt I was seeing it in action. My father's cruel deeds had rebounded on him and he was paying for them now. He was experiencing his guilt and it was very sad to see.

My experiences over the years have led me to conclude that when we die we leave our earthly bodies and walk away from them accompanied by a loved one who has already made the journey. If we've lived good lives we join our old families and friends in that beautiful place the Lined Man showed me when I was a child. But if we have hurt people and done things we know we shouldn't have done then the true knowledge of the effects of our behaviour suddenly hits us and we truly understand the pain we have caused. Sometimes this feels so bad the person concerned is too ashamed to go with his loved ones and stays hanging around the earth in misery. I can see where the Catholic idea of Purgatory comes from.

As for God, He fits in there somewhere. Maybe overseeing the whole process from on high.

Despite all he'd done I didn't actually hate my father and I couldn't bear to watch any more. As soon as the funeral finished, Peter and I hurried away.

That wasn't quite the end. Several times after that my

father came to me in dreams, haunted looking and desperate. 'I can't seem to find my way,' he kept saying, 'I can't find my way to the right place.' And then he'd shake his head and walk off.

Mum dreamed of him too. Apparently he kept asking her to forgive him and she said she couldn't.

'Did I do the right thing, Diane?' she asked, troubled. 'Is that too harsh? Because when I think back to what he did to me, I can't forgive him.'

'I don't know Mum,' I said. 'You can only say what you feel.'

It was all very sad and yet as the weeks passed I began to feel that a shadow had lifted from my life. Somehow, even though I hadn't seen him for years, it was if my father had hovered like an unlucky ghost over my relationships with men. Whenever anything went wrong in my marriage or my partnership, it reminded me of him. And now he'd gone it was almost as if a curse had been lifted. Peter and I were free to build whatever relationship we could achieve in our own right, without being dragged down by the past.

We both continued working hard and neither of us was in a rush to get married. We'd been through so much together we were secure in the knowledge that we were meant to be, and that's all that mattered.

I was still baffled by the psychic powers that I seemed to possess and I was keen to discover the extent of what I could do and where my limits might lie. So one day, when I was at home confined to bed with flu, I turned on the TV and a programme with medium Derek

Acorah came on. He was demonstrating his skills by tuning in to random members of the audience and amazing everyone with the information he discovered. I was pretty bored with being ill, so just for fun I thought I'd have a go along with him. When Derek tuned in, I tuned in, and despite the fact that I was miles away in Wales I was delighted to find that I was getting the same details about his volunteer as he was right next to them in the studio.

It was incredibly satisfying – rather like joining in with one of those TV quiz shows at home and finding that you know all the answers. By the time the pro-gramme finished I was thinking to myself, 'I could do this. I could be on TV.'

It seemed a crazy idea and I wasn't really sure I wanted to be on TV but the notion kept nagging at me. 'Phone them. Phone them,' cousin Peter kept saying in my ear.

So when I was feeling a little better I looked up the telephone number of the TV company and rang them.

'You know, I can do the sort of thing that Derek Acorah was doing,' I said when I eventually got to talk to the producer of the show *Granada Breeze*. 'I wouldn't mind coming up and taking a chance; doing a chal-lenge, a sort of blind date challenge. You could put someone behind a screen so that I couldn't see them. I wouldn't even know if it was a man or a woman and then no-one could say I was guessing information from their appearance.'

Even though I knew that cousin Peter was pushing me in this direction I still half expected them to say 'no', but they didn't.

'Okay,' said the producer, 'Come on up to Manchester and we'll see what you can do.'

I was a nervous wreck on the way up there in the car. Peter's mum gave me a very expensive suit to wear from the clothes shop she ran and I'd spent hours fiddling with my hair but I still felt awful and desperately sick. To make matters worse, I'd long realised that I needed to keep my stomach empty before I worked – it's as if I have to direct every available drop of blood to my brain rather than my tummy – so I never eat beforehand, but this policy had left me with a gnawing emptiness inside that was almost painful.

In the event though, cousin Peter and the Lined Man didn't let me down. While we were still on the motorway they told me that my challenge was going to be a girl, not a boy, that she'd been having trouble with her TV aerial and she was going to Frankfurt to live.

Sure enough, when the cameras started rolling I relayed this information and more, and it seemed to be correct. The only thing the girl couldn't place was the bit about Frankfurt. Just for good measure, afterwards I was talking to Louisa, the researcher, and I saw her mother standing behind her. I described her mum and then I added, 'Your mum says you've got a restaurant.' Which turned out to be true. She also said that Louisa would shortly be working across the road from where she was now, and a few months later Louisa moved across to the other studios which were located opposite.

The experiment was judged to be such a success that I was invited back to do it again. It's funny the way things snowball. The local papers picked up snippets about my TV appearances and TV companies picked up snippets about me from the newspaper stories, and soon I was being invited onto more TV shows and onto radio programmes and then, of course, the reporters wanted to interview me all over again.

By now I didn't get so nervous but I was rather bemused by it all. I tended to accept almost everything that came along just to see where it might lead. So when I was invited over to Dublin to chat on a TV show and give a talk at the R.D.S. centre (a big conference hall rather like the NEC in Birmingham), it seemed like a wonderful excuse to see a beautiful city I'd never visited before and have a little break. Peter was too busy to get away from work, but Mum agreed to come with me and we were looking forward to staying in a hotel and having a real girls' weekend.

Just before I was due to leave, a reporter rang to talk about the show and there was something about her voice that made strange images come into my head. I saw a pretty young girl with long fair hair and she'd been murdered. 'I was only two minutes from home,' the girl said. The killer had not been found and she didn't think this was right.

'I know the case you're talking about,' said the

reporter. 'There's been lot of interest in it here, but I don't think there've been many leads.'

I mentioned a few other details that the girl asked me to pass on, but once I put the phone down I didn't think about it again. I was much too busy packing my case, getting the children organised and calling for Mum.

The wonderful thing about the trip was that we could fly straight from Swansea airport and I was looking forward to it. Yet when I glanced in the mirror to check my hair as I walked out of the door my heart sank. The glass misted over before my eyes in a way that was becoming depressingly familiar.

'Oh no,' I thought. 'What's going to go wrong now?'

I peered at it again but it was still the same and I could only see myself as a vague blur through the haze. But there was nothing I could do about it. We had a plane to catch.

Mum is a bit of a nervous flyer and she likes a drink before she can force herself to climb on board, so when we got to the airport she made straight for the bar. I don't normally drink in the middle of the day, but that cloud in the mirror had unsettled me so much I joined her in a vodka and coke to calm my nerves.

Then the flight was called and we made our way to one of the smallest commercial planes I'd ever seen – a tiny toy-like craft that only held about 19 passengers. Mum regarded it dubiously and, although I knew it was the wrong thing to say, I couldn't help confiding, 'I don't think this plane is going to take off.'

Mum turned even paler. 'Now don't you start! Don't you start, Diane! I don't want to know.'

But there was something wrong and I knew it, although I could hardly say anything when I had no evidence of any problems at all.

We strapped ourselves into our seats, the engines started up and the little plane swung round and began to taxi up the runway.

'There's something wrong with the right side of the engine,' I told Mum. 'We're not going to get off the ground.' Yet I wasn't too frightened. My inner voices were saying 'Don't worry. Everything's going to work out.'

Mum gave a little moan and shut her eyes. The plane gathered speed and we roared along, faster and faster towards the horizon, and then, instead of lifting off, the note of the engines abruptly changed. We slowed and turned round.

'There's been a slight problem, ladies and gentlemen,' came the pilot's voice over the address system, 'and we'll be returning to the terminal for a few minutes. Sorry for any inconvenience.'

'Oh my God, Diane,' said Mum. 'You've done it again.'

And we were back at the airport.

As we were walking into the building we saw the pilot striding ahead of us and Mum, being Mum, went up to him and said: 'My daughter's psychic and she sensed there was something wrong with the right side of the engine. Can you sort it out please?'

The pilot looked at her as if he suspected she might be a little crazy but he smiled politely.

'We'll certainly do our best, madam.' And off he went.

I got Mum into the café and bought her a cup of tea, but it wasn't long before she'd fallen into conversation with another visitor to the airport, a tall, gentlemanly figure with fair hair, bright blue eyes and an almost military bearing. He turned out to be a retired police-man called Peter Hall who now worked freelance as a cameraman for HTV television. He'd come to the airport that day to investigate some psychic phenomena believed to date from World War II.

Naturally, Mum had to regale him with the whole engine story. I'm not sure Peter was completely con-vinced, but as we were talking the pilot appeared again and headed straight for me.

'You were right, love!' he said in quite a different tone to the one he'd used with Mum before. 'How did you know about the engine? And are we going to be able to take off this time?'

'Yes,' I said, laughing. 'There'll be no more problems now.'

'I'm very glad to hear it,' he said. 'We could do with you on board *every* day.'

Peter Hall was intrigued.

'Maybe we could work together some time,' he said. 'We might get something on film.'

'Certainly,' I said, as we hurried away to re-board the plane. 'Give me a call when I get back.'

And then we were off once more and this time we got

to Dublin without a hitch. But though I didn't know it then, the problem with the plane was only the beginning of the excitement.

Mum and I arrived at the TV studios without further mishap and I did my little talk with the presenter, but as I was walking out of the studios, three faintly sinister looking men accosted me. One was a real Irish redhead, one was short and plump and one was thin and dark.

'Are you Diane Lloyd Hughes?' they asked in solemn, rather scary tones.

That was the married name I still retained.

'Yes,' I said.

'We're detectives and we need to speak to you. Now.'

Mum went white. She thought I was being arrested, but before I could find out what on earth was going on I was being marched out to their car and ushered briskly into the back seat.

They climbed in around me and one of them tossed a newspaper onto my lap.

'You're taking a chance there aren't you?' said the dark-haired one.

I had no idea what he was talking about, but when I looked down at the newspaper I saw that the reporter I'd spoken to before I came away had written a dramatic story based on our conversation. Readers were informed that I'd come up with new clues about the unsolved murder case which had happened a year or so before and I was visiting Ireland to see what else I could discover.

'The murderer's still at large,' said the red-haired

detective. 'You could be his next victim. You're taking quite a risk coming out with stuff like that.'

My stomach turned over. Put like that I did feel a bit stupid. Such a thought had never entered my head, but on the other hand that poor girl deserved justice. If everyone with possible information was too frightened to speak out, no crime would ever be solved.

'Well, now you're here let's see what you can pick up,' said the dark-haired detective.

I sensed a tide of scepticism swirling around me so I tried to give them some little details that they might recognise that would reassure them I wasn't a fantasist.

'You're wearing your Christmas coat,' I said to the thin dark man.

He looked blank. 'I don't know what you mean,' he said.

So I tried the plump man. 'And you've got loads of unfinished books in the boot of your car.'

'You're wrong there love,' he said.

I sighed dejectedly. This was turning into a nightmare.

Mum meanwhile was in a terrible panic. She'd been bundled into another car. No-one had thought to explain what was going on and she imagined I'd been arrested on suspicion of heaven knows what awful crime. It must be serious if it took three detectives to apprehend me she reasoned.

While Mum worried and thought the worst, I was being driven to a leafy part of town.

'Okay,' said the detectives when we finally drew up in

a pleasant street of comfortable houses. 'Why don't you take a walk around here a bit and do what you do.'

So I climbed out and looked around. There was a lane and some trees and a small wall. The same girl as before came close to me as I stood there. I could feel her hair swinging round her face and see her eyes all pretty with make-up. I wanted to walk towards the lane.

'I had a sister and a brother,' she told me.

Then I had an impression of several carrier bags. She was holding carrier bags as if she'd been shopping earlier. I could feel them knocking lightly against my legs and cutting into my fingers as I walked. Suddenly a young man appeared from behind a tree. He'd been waiting there for her. He knew her. I saw him pulling at the carrier bags. 'What have you bought now?' he was demanding nastily. 'What have you bought now?'

Then there was a stinging sensation as a knife sliced over her arm again and again followed by a terrible pain in my side. When I put my hand to my side my fingers felt wet with blood.

'She's been stabbed!' I gasped. 'In the side.'

But the girl was pulling at me again and she directed my eyes to the little wall where shocked neighbours had placed bunches of memorial flowers, obviously some while ago because the sad little posies were all blackened and dead.

'The flowers are in the wrong place,' said the girl.

I mentioned this to the detectives and then I followed the girl to a spot a short distance away where I saw her body was slumped.

'This is where they should have put the flowers,' I said. 'This is where she was found. She was trying to crawl home.' And as I spoke I had a sudden image of a guilty hand cleaning a knife and then cunningly putting it away beside other blameless domestic knives in a kitchen drawer.

'The knife is back in a kitchen drawer,' I said. 'It's still being used in the killer's kitchen.'

The detectives gave nothing away. It was only later I found out that 17-year-old Raonaid Murray had been stabbed, exactly as I described, on her way home from the pub on September 4 1999. Tragically, her body was found by her older sister shortly afterwards.

They took me back to my mother who was red-eyed and frantic, but they still hadn't finished with us. Instead of driving us to our hotel they whisked us back to the police station where they threw dozens and dozens of photographs of possible suspects at me.

'Is that him?' they asked. 'What about him?' and so on and so on until I was so exhausted I could hardly see. Yet the killer was not in the pictures. I didn't feel he was previously known to the police.

When they'd finally finished, they announced we couldn't even go to the hotel where we'd booked a room.

'We've moved you for your own security,' they said.

Mind you, we didn't care when we saw the alternative accommodation they'd found for us. They drove us to the smart Conrad Hotel on the edge of town, where the manager had allocated us the penthouse suite. It was beautiful but I was too tired to appreciate it just then. I fell into bed, completely shattered, and cried my eyes out. It was partly tiredness and partly the dreadful things that Raonaid had shown me.

To this day the killer hasn't been found, but I'm convinced that his family know who he is and are shielding him. Perhaps one day they'll realise that their silence is not the answer to anything. It's not fair to Raonaid and in the long run it won't help the guilty man. He's still got to pay for his crimes, as he'll find out one day soon enough. Just like my father did.

The next morning the detectives appeared again and this time they were in a much more friendly mood. Apparently the details I'd given them were correct. They'd even gone back with tape measures and marked out from their records exactly where the body had been found. The place corresponded with the spot I'd indicated. I gathered that none of these details had yet been publicised, so they were intrigued as to how I could have known. What's more, both the dark-haired detective and the plump detective had made small but strange personal discoveries after they left me.

In his rush to leave home the day we met, the dark-haired detective had grabbed the wrong coat from the hook in his hall. Instead of the work coat he'd intended to put on, he'd picked up the new coat his daughter had given him for Christmas. He didn't even realise his mistake till he got back that night.

As for the plump detective, he went to fetch something from the boot of his car and as he rummaged around through a pile of other items he noticed an old box hidden at the back. When he looked inside he found a forgotten stack of books he'd intended to read but never finished.

They were both pretty gobsmacked.

Chapter Seventeen

One spring morning in 2002 a middle-aged woman came to me for a reading. Her name was Myron and she lived in Swansea, but as usual I didn't ask her what she was hoping for, I just let my guides step in and lead me where I needed to go.

Myron settled herself comfortably in the office chair I keep for guests and I concentrated on her as usual. There was no hint that this reading would be anything out of the ordinary, it was just another day as far as I was concerned.

Almost immediately, two figures appeared behind Myron on the part of my office wall that I leave plain especially for this purpose – my psychic wall screen as it were. They were standing close in the way that family members do. One was a tall, sweet-faced girl with a shy smile, the other was a young man in a denim jacket.

'I'm Sian,' said the girl, and when I mentioned this to Myron she seemed very pleased.

'That's my daughter,' she said. 'She was killed in a car accident.'

'And the young man is called Mark,' I went on.

'I was murdered,' Mark was saying over the top of Myron's head. 'Ask Myron to tell my parents.'

This sounded worrying. Surely Mark's parents knew if he was murdered? Or could it be they thought his death was an accident? There wasn't a tactful way of putting this so I just came out with it.

'And Mark was murdered.'

Myron turned pale and her hands flew to her mouth.

'No! No, he's just gone missing.' She was clearly shocked but Mark was insisting that Myron be told the truth.

'I'm sorry,' I said gently, 'but Mark is dead too and he's been murdered. He wants his parents to know and he wants his killers found.'

It turned out that Mark Green was Myron's nephew. He was a college lecturer from Birmingham and he'd gone out one night in the middle of January, two months before, for a few drinks with a friend. No-one had seen him since.

Apparently, during the evening the friend had felt unwell and gone home early, leaving Mark in a club finishing his drink. Afterwards Mark was picked up by CCTV cameras as he wandered out into the street, then he walked up the road, disappeared out of range and seemingly vanished off the face of the earth. When he didn't come home, his worried parents rang the police because this behaviour was so out of character.

'If he stayed over with friends he always phoned to let us know where he was,' his mother said later. 'That's why we knew something had happened. Being inconsiderate like that just wasn't in his nature.'

But despite a massive police investigation and public appeal for information there were no positive leads. No-one could even say whether Mark was dead or alive. Of course we often hear stories of people who can't cope with their lives any more, and who disappear without trace to start afresh in a different place under a different name, but Myron had never believed that such a caring man as Mark would do something so hurtful. She feared the worst.

'I always thought Mark would never come home,' she told me after getting over the horror of having her suspicions confirmed.

'Well, it's all going to come out,' I went on. 'He's mentioned a woman with short dark hair who's helping to find him . . .'

'That must be Marcella. Marcella Daly, the detective who's looking into the case,' said Myron.

'And there's going to be a television programme about his disappearance,' I added. 'Shortly after that broadcast, Mark's body will be found.'

I don't suppose Myron enjoyed her sitting, it was too distressing, but she was impressed enough to take the tape recording she'd made of my words to Detective Constable Daly of the Birmingham police who was investigating the case.

When she listened to it – DC Daly admitted later – she was stunned. 'At the time we'd been selective about what we put in the press,' Marcella told reporters,

'When I listened to the tape I was certain that no-one could have known the things Diane came up with. Particularly details about the circumstances in which Mark left the nightclub, his appearance and mood. None of that had been divulged to the public.'

Not long afterwards, DC Daly phoned me and asked if I'd be willing to come to Birmingham to retrace Mark's last known steps, in the hope that I could throw any more light on his disappearance.

I was beginning to understand what I was in for when I agreed to get involved in murder cases and I knew it wouldn't be pleasant. Yet Mark badly wanted me to do it. He knew that his parents couldn't rest until his body was found and he desperately wanted to help them in the only way now open to him. If his parents could grieve properly, then maybe they could move on with the rest of their lives.

'Certainly,' I told Marcella Daly, 'I'll be glad to do whatever I can.'

As soon as I arrived, feeling extremely nervous, at the club where Mark was last seen, Mark himself appeared on the pavement beside me, still wearing his denim jacket.

'I want to help the police find them,' he said. 'Come on. Come with me, I'll show you the way.' He started moving off down the road, so I hurried after him, two policemen with a tape recorder following in my wake.

For nearly two hours we combed those cold, grey streets with Mark getting increasingly agitated as he led us along towards the place where he was murdered. He wanted to do this, but reliving that night was distressing for him. Suddenly he stopped and a great wave of nausea swept into my stomach.

A series of horrifying pictures unreeled in my mind. I saw a man lift a big metal canister and smash it over Mark's head. His knees buckled and he fell to the floor, but then he was being kicked, kicked in the head. After a while he lay still, but there was another man there and they hadn't finished with him yet. There was a flash of silver blades going through flesh and the smell of blood. They were cutting up his body, cutting it up into small pieces and the pieces were shoved into black bin liners. For some reason it looked as if the body was under water. It was somewhere dark and murky.

I felt sick to the soles of my feet. I'd seen enough. With a wrench I forced the scene out of my mind just as Jeff had taught me all those years ago. I tried to visualise things that had nothing to do with the case – the railway station where I'd be going as soon as this was over, what I'd have for tea that night. Anything but the pictures of horror that had been played out in my mind.

'It happened around here,' I told the police, 'you'll find his body in black bin bags somewhere close. I can see his body under water somehow.'

I was exhausted and I knew that I'd given an accurate description of what happened. Yet frustratingly, though they searched the whole area very thoroughly, the police could find no trace of the bin bags or any other incriminating evidence.

There was nothing else I could do but go home and wait. Nearly three months passed, but then a programme about missing people was screened and the baffling case of Mark Green was aired once more.

Astonishingly, just after the show, the police got a call from a young man named James McMahon who had seen the programme and couldn't bear to live with his conscience any longer. He told them that his brother Robert had killed and then dismembered Mark's body in his Birmingham flat which just happened to be close by the spot where I'd seen those disturbing images.

They'd placed the body parts in black bin liners, hidden them in suitcases and then taken them by taxi to James's home some distance away, where they buried them in the garden.

Just as Mark had predicted, his body was found shortly after the screening of a TV programme about his disappearance. It was somewhere dark and murky all right, though not under water. I'm still puzzled about that. Maybe James's garden flooded from time to time or perhaps they buried the bin bags in a boggy patch. I don't know. I can only say what I saw.

In April 2004 Robert McMahon, aged 24, was jailed for Mark's murder and his brother James, 21, was sentenced to two years for helping to dispose of Mark's body.

Thankfully not all my cases were so harrowing. Some are really delightful. One woman was thrilled when I saw lottery numbers and loads of money coming her way. Greatly encouraged by this she started doing the lottery and two weeks later she won several thousand pounds.

Another woman was down in the dumps because her family had grown up, she had many talents but she didn't seem able to pursue them. Yet on my office wall I could see a book with her name on it arriving from the publisher's. When I mentioned this she said that she was indeed writing a book but couldn't see it ever getting published.

'It will be,' I assured her, and eventually it was.

I learned a lot from the people I met. I began to build up a fuller picture of the unseen world that is so close to ours and yet is so difficult to understand.

I'll never forget the day I was reading the paper and saw a photograph of a boy called Lee who was in a coma. He'd suffered head injuries in a car accident and he'd been unconscious for three months. So long, in fact, that the doctors were certain he wouldn't live and they were going to switch off the life support machine.

I finished the story, shook my head at the sadness of it all and was just turning the page the way we all do, when a woman's voice said loudly in my ear: 'They can't turn the machine off, he's going to survive. He's going to live.'

Involuntarily I looked over my shoulder, but of course there was no-one there. However, even though I couldn't see her, the lady, who I took to be Lee's grandmother, was extremely worried about the situation and she didn't intend to let Lee slip away.

'He's good boy,' she told me, 'He used to come to my house and have sandwiches all the time. You've got to ring up and stop them turning that machine off.'

I have to admit I was dismayed. How could I convince the hospital to listen to me? They'd think I was a crank. But the grandmother kept nagging me. What did making a fool of yourself matter when there was a life at stake? She had a point, of course, and in the end I rang the hospital.

'Could I possibly speak to the woman who's the mother of that boy in a coma?' I asked.

'Are you a relative?' asked the receptionist.

'Um no,' I said, feeling even more of an idiot. I explained briefly who I was. 'I know it sounds crazy but I've got a very important message for Lee's mother. Could you ask her if she'd like to talk to me? And if she would, she can ring me.'

'Okay,' said the woman dubiously, 'I'll pass the message on.'

A few minutes later Susan, Lee's mother, called me back.

'Thank you for ringing,' I said. 'I hope you don't mind me telling you this but I've got an old lady here who says she's your mum and that her grandson who used to come to her house for sandwiches a lot is on a life-support machine and they mustn't turn it off.'

Then another voice came into my head. It was a young man's voice. 'They keep putting something in my hand,' said the young man, 'and I don't like it. Tell them to stop.'

Susan gasped. 'How do you know these things? That's a private room. No-one else can go in there.'

'Lee's telling me,' I said, 'I don't know how. I think it must be that even people in a coma can sort of float out of their body and talk to people like me. But he wants you to know you mustn't turn the machine off. There's a specialist in Cardiff who can help him. Don't let them turn off that machine. He's going to survive and he's going to call you Mam again.'

Susan clearly didn't know what to think. She said she'd keep an open mind and thanked me for taking the trouble to call. But a few hours later she phoned me back, much more excited.

'I was talking to my daughter, Andrea, and told her what you'd said,' she said, 'and apparently while I was talking to you, Andrea had been at Lee's bedside and she kept running a piece of silk through Lee's hands to try to get a reaction. There was no reaction but Lee wouldn't have liked it – he hates the feel of silk.'

After that, from time to time over the weeks, Lee would come back and give me messages for his mum which I passed on. Oddly enough I always seemed to phone at just the moment there'd been an upset. One day when I caught Susan she was quite distressed because she'd just had a call from a tearful Andrea.

'Andrea couldn't bear it because she'd spent so long with Lee and she felt he didn't know she was there,' said Susan.

'He does,' I explained. 'He's holding up a packet of cigarettes to me and he's saying he'd have liked one too.

{ 273 }

Also he says that there was a loud bang that startled the whole ward.'

When Susan checked with Andrea it turned out that Andrea had bought a packet of cigarettes for her boyfriend and gave them to him while they were in the ward. Also, while clearing up the top of Lee's locker she'd accidentally knocked two heavy metal Chinese therapy balls onto the floor which made quite a crash.

Basically, I think Lee wanted his family to know that there was hope and that they mustn't give up. Against all the odds he did eventually regain consciousness and, though it took several years, he did call Susan 'Mam' again.

The idea of being able to talk to people who are in a coma continued to seem unbelievable until just a little while ago when I read an interesting report in the papers. Doctors had scanned the brain of a coma patient who appeared to be completely unresponsive in every way, but when they talked of playing tennis and other activities, the area of her brain that would be active when undertaking sport, lit up. It seemed that she could not only hear and understand them, she could also imagine herself playing the very game they described.

Other cases made me think in different ways. During a reading with one woman I was concerned to learn that she was about to suffer a serious problem with her leg. She was going to be okay but there was nothing I could do to prevent this happening. I had to be content with reassuring her that this was only a blip in her life and she mustn't worry. She went away imagining a broken leg or something of that sort.

A few months later she phoned to tell me what had actually happened. While she was driving down the motorway one day, a car had suddenly veered across the opposite carriageway, gone straight through the central reservation, and smashed into her. Her own vehicle crumpled all around her, trapping her inside, the wreckage entangling her leg.

The fire brigade rushed to her aid and were frantically trying to cut her free, but she could feel her blood pumping out of the gash and she was slipping away.

'Stay awake, love. Stay with us. Don't close your eyes,' the firemen kept telling her. 'Come on, stay awake.'

And she turned her head and saw her father sitting beside her on the previously empty passenger seat.

'Yes, love. Do what they say. Stay awake,' he said.

She said she tried as hard as she could, but in the end she was so tired she decided to close her eyes just for a second. Instantly her father was there right in front of her and he put a warning hand up to her face.

'No!' he said. 'You're not coming with me. It's not your time yet. Go back.'

She opened her eyes again and a few moments later her leg was free and she was being rushed to hospital. She made a full recovery and now she has no doubt that when it really is her time, her dad will come for her and she has no need to fear.

Sometimes I see things that can't be changed and

believe there is no point in telling people things that would upset them. It's distressing for me but I understand now that it's part of the job.

And then there're guardian angels. My friend Wendy is a great believer in angels and after a holiday in Corfu she was left in no doubt that her own personal angel is close at hand.

Wendy and her boyfriend were having a wonderful holiday on the Greek island and they were so enthusiastic they booked themselves up for practically every trip on offer. There was just one that seemed to elude them. They were tempted by a mini cruise to an unspoiled bay that could only be reached from the sea, where they could picnic on the beach and swim from the boat. It seemed idyllic, but the first day they tried to book the boat was full. The second day, they arrived at the ticket office to find Wendy's boyfriend had forgotten his credit card and couldn't pay. Finally, they bought tickets for the next morning and left their hotel bright and early to catch the bus to the harbour. They waited patiently for some time at the stop, only to see the bus sail straight past them without even slowing. Wendy began to get a very bad feeling about this trip.

'I don't think we're supposed to go,' she said.

Her boyfriend wasn't having any of such superstitious nonsense.

'Don't be silly,' he said. 'After we've gone to so much trouble to get on this trip we can't give up now. We'll get a taxi.'

Mixed Blessings

So they took a taxi to the harbour and boarded their boat, but as they walked along the gang plank Wendy sent a silent prayer to her guardian angel: 'Please put a cloak of protection round us.' Wendy told her boyfriend, he laughed and walked on.

The excursion was glorious. The sun shone, the sea was calm and the coastline spectacular. Eventually they moored just outside a little bay for swimming in the warm blue water. Wendy jumped in and when she surfaced she turned to wave at her boyfriend who was still on the deck. But, instead of laughing and waving back, his face was aghast and he was making frantic signals for her to return.

Wendy glanced over her shoulder and was horrified to see another boat hurtling at full speed straight towards the pleasure cruiser and she was right in its path. She didn't know whether to veer left, right or attempt to swim for the cruiser. In the end she made for the cruiser, the out of control boat right behind her. Somehow she reached the metal steps before she was mown down but, instead of climbing them, she tucked herself in behind them. The next second the boat slammed into the hull of the cruiser, knocking several passengers into the sea and making quite a dent. Had Wendy been on the steps she could have been killed. As it was they protected her from the impact. Or, as Wendy puts it, her angel protected her.

In fact, I believe we've all got guardian angels. I think they're either very good people who've passed on but come back to look after individuals, or sometimes they're past members of our own family who love us very much and want to stay around to help.

I don't think we ask our angels for help often enough. Personally, every time I get into my car these days I ask my angel to look after me while I'm driving. You've only got to ask!

Angels often appear when medical help is needed. I've only seen my angel once. I woke up early one morning to see a beautiful being full of light in the bedroom.

'You need a small operation,' it said, 'don't worry, but be prepared.'

I felt fine but not long afterwards I needed some minor surgery on a dental matter.

My psychic work had really taken off in a big way and I was spending so much time doing readings, healing, going out and about on criminal cases or visiting TV or radio stations that cooking in the tearoom was becoming impossible to fit in. I missed making my scones and fancy cakes because I so enjoyed being up to my arms in flour and creating tasty things – but I realised that the time had come to give up Sweet Memories.

I loved it – it was my baby – but if I couldn't give it the care it deserved then it would be better to let some-one else take over. Two women approached me with a view to running a café on the site and I decided to let them try their luck.

Other things were changing, too. During the summer – through my readings – I'd met a few people who were keen to develop their psychic powers; something every-one can do. They were from all walks of life: one was a doctor, one a stripper, one a priest and one an old spiritualist. I'd agreed to run through some of the exercises Jeff had taught me, and after a few lessons one of them startled me by coming out with a prediction for me.

'You're going to be getting married before the year's out, Di,' they said.

Since it was already June and Peter and I had no plans, I thought this was highly unlikely. Yet deep down I did have a suspicion I'd remarry one day because I'd seen a sudden picture of myself in a white dress, carrying flowers on a beautiful Caribbean beach. I'd never been to the Caribbean before but I got the strong impression that I was going through a wedding ceremony there.

Then one day Peter surprised me by coming home and announcing that we could both do with a holiday and he'd booked us a break in Barbados in November. Who wouldn't be excited about a winter holiday in the sun? I was delighted, especially when he showed me the brochure and the gorgeous hotel he'd chosen.

Not long after this it was my birthday and Peter whisked me off for dinner at a very swish hotel called Morgans in Swansea. It was a beautiful evening, Peter ordered drinks and as the glasses were put in front of us I looked over Peter's shoulder and saw what looked like fireworks going off. They weren't real, they were psychic fireworks, firing off across the wall behind him.

How odd! I thought. Peter's very excited about something. It was my birthday of course but surely the fireworks feeling was a bit over the top.

'Come on, Diane, have your drink!' said Peter eagerly and I saw another brilliant rocket whoosh off behind him.

I picked up my glass and took a sip. Peter seemed a bit disappointed.

'Have some more, go on!' he said.

And that's when I looked down and saw something odd about the ice cube that was floating in my glass. There was something frozen into the centre of it. Carefully I prised it out of the glass and there suspended in the ice was a beautiful diamond solitaire ring.

'I thought we'd go for the wedding package in Barbados!' said Peter. 'What d'you think?'

Tears filled my eyes.

'I think that's a wonderful idea,' I said, taking his hand.

We'd always known that we'd stay together, of course, and sort of assumed that one day we'd get married, but with two broken relationships behind me I was in no rush. Now I realised that this was in fact the perfect moment.

It was only later that I realised the particular package Peter had booked didn't include a beach wedding. The ceremony was conducted at the hotel – not, as my vision had suggested, on a beach. Still, why quibble? My vision was obviously wrong for once.

The arrangements were a bit of a rush but I found a

sophisticated white evening dress that was perfect, and, though arranging a wedding so far from home meant that our family and friends would not be able to join us, we organised another service and party in Wales for them when we got back in December.

The ceremony was booked for November 18 and to my astonishment we discovered when we arrived on the island that, although it hadn't been mentioned in the brochure, there was actually a beach option available.

'We've got to go for the beach, Peter,' I said in delight. 'It's meant to be.'

So the beach it was. I was given away by a friend of Peter's – the charming Barbadian cricketer, Desmond Haynes. He walked through the village to the beach with me on his arm, joking with everyone we met: 'This is my new wife!'

And then finally, under the blazing Barbados sky, with the waves breaking on the beach, I enjoyed the perfect wedding, to my perfect man.

Chapter Eighteen

I had a wedding ring on my finger, I was a 'Mrs' again and I'd moved into new premises behind the shops opposite my old tearoom. I was very sad to see Sweet Memories becoming just a sweet memory, but I was pleased that I'd followed my dream, made it come true and got it out of my system. It was as if the spirit world was allowing me to have a go at what I wanted to do so that I wouldn't look back in regret when I found myself doing what *they* wanted me to do.

I couldn't complain that full-time psychic work was dull. The variety was astonishing. I've never considered myself a history buff but I even ended up at an archaeological site, thanks to Peter's receptionist Liz.

I was overloaded with paperwork and she popped in from time to time to give me a hand. Liz was fascinated by history and when she read that the remains of a medieval ship had been discovered on the banks of the River Usk, near Newport, she wondered what psychic details I might be able to pick up from the wreck.

It seemed highly unlikely to me that I'd be allowed anywhere near the fragile boat, but Liz can be very persuasive. She contacted the Mary Rose Trust, who were working on the ship, and they agreed that I could go along and examine it.

We drove to the big warehouse where teams of scientists and archaeologists were examining the ship in painstaking detail. I say 'ship', but when we were escorted inside I saw no ship, just dozens of bright yellow plastic baths filled with water in which lay rotting pieces of timber. The vessel was now reduced to 1,700 melancholy fragments.

It didn't look too promising, but I was issued with rubber gloves and allowed to dip my fingers gently into one of the baths. Instantly I was standing on the deck of a creaking wooden boat, watching green hills bobbing past. A small boy with blond curls was crouched on his hands and knees on the deck, scrubbing, and I heard the date 1426. The cracks between the planks were filled with some black substance which seemed to be a mixture of hair and tar and when the boy stood up he had big calluses on his knees and hands.

He told me there were 35 people on board the boat and that it sank because it was overloaded. It was the fault of the Earl, the boy told me. Apparently, this Earl arranged for illegal cargoes of silverware and crockery to be carried between Newport and Bristol, and one day his greed led him to load too much cargo on board.

I had a last glimpse of an expensively dressed man who looked like a pirate with big gold buttons on his clothes.

Liz discovered from the archaeologists afterwards that the boat had sunk in 1451 and that my descriptions of the way the timbers were made watertight were accurate. It seemed that around this time the Earl of Warwick financed his many ambitions by piracy and owned a small fleet of ships which operated in the area to make money for him in this way.

Liz was thrilled by my accuracy.

My old friend Peter Hall, the policeman-turned-TV-cameraman, was keen to see what I could do too, and he phoned one afternoon to tell me he had an old unsolved case for me to get my teeth into. Naturally, he wouldn't say anything else about it.

It was a cold, wintry morning when Peter took me to a remote spot in the country near an overgrown lane. There were steep banks on either side and the trees met overhead to create a tunnel. It made me shiver just looking at it. We began walking and straight away I heard a sweet voice singing. Then I saw a little girl with a bow in her hair. She told me she was 12, though she looked about nine, and her name was Muriel.

I could see green leaves on the trees, so it wasn't winter, but Muriel was showing me a pixie hat, a pair of gloves and a blue school mac.

'It was cold and I thought it was going to rain,' said Muriel.

She kept talking about selling oranges and eggs, which seemed a bit odd. Then I saw the figure of a man beside her from the back. I got the impression she knew him. She'd certainly seen him before.

Then the situation rapidly became horrific. Muriel was dragged into a nearby field and raped.

I started to shake and tears came into my eyes. I didn't want to see what I was seeing. The man abused her horribly, then he stabbed her and the next thing I knew he'd pulled out a gun and shot her.

'Surely she wasn't stabbed *and* shot?' I asked Peter in distress.

He couldn't give me any answers then, but later I discovered that this had been the case.

'I think this man got away with it and he's still alive,' I said, 'I'd say he's from a farming background and he still lives here in Wales. And Muriel knew him.'

The case was so upsetting I vowed that I'd never do anything like it ever again. Whenever I closed my eyes I was haunted by the sight of those poor, defenceless, little bare white legs.

Peter recorded the whole episode on camera and made a DVD of my information. Afterwards he told me what was known about poor little Muriel. It seemed the nice little girl with the bow in her hair had a beautiful singing voice and was known locally as the Little Nightingale. She was called Muriel Drinkwater and she lived on a farm. She used to walk through the woods to the bus stop on her way to school every morning and she often helped her mother by selling eggs and other items along the way. On June 27 1946 she left for school as usual but she never came home. Her body was found dumped in woodland. She'd been raped, shot and stabbed. Despite a massive hunt, the killer was never found.

It seemed that no matter what I did, I couldn't escape

such sadness. Even my healing, which usually produced happy results, sometimes led in the opposite direction. There are times when you'd really rather not know what the future holds, and I began to see that the ability people often regard as a gift can just as often feel like a curse.

The case of a lovely young woman called Jane was a particularly vivid example. Jane's sister had met my mum by chance and when she heard that Mum was related to a psychic who was also a healer she wondered if I might able to help her sister Jane, who had been very ill.

'I'm sure Diane'd be only too pleased,' said Mum and promptly arranged for me to make a visit.

I arrived at Jane's neat little terraced house the next day and was shown into the sitting room. It was a bustling, family place with photos of two little boys and a girl dotted about. This was a happy home if ever I'd seen one. The next second Jane herself came in. She didn't look ill at all. She had long blonde hair, a pretty face and a bright, bubbly personality. This was surely going to be an easy case, I thought.

But as Jane sat down and I put my hands on her shoulders, ready to start healing, I felt a sort of jolt. Instead of the tingling heat burning into my hands that normally comes when I'm healing, I was seeing pictures instead, pictures that I had no wish to look at. I saw a funeral, I saw a hearse submerged in flowers driving away from Jane's house and dozens and dozens of weeping people . . . It was Jane's funeral. She was going to die. She had liver cancer and it had spread.

It was so awful I wanted to snatch my hands off her shoulders and walk away, walk right out of that house and never come back. But I couldn't. I couldn't take away her hope.

Hovering close by I sensed the presence of an older woman. It was Jane's grandmother and in desperation I appealed to her.

'Help her please!' I begged silently. 'Don't let this happen. You can stop it.'

But the grandmother shook her head. 'I'm sorry, I can't help her. This is what's going to happen. She has to come back.'

I was devastated and my hands dropped from Jane's back.

'All finished?' asked Jane brightly, twisting round to look at me. 'That was really relaxing. Did you feel anything?'

'I saw your grandmother,' I said weakly. I had to say something.

'Really?' said Jane. 'You know, I've always felt I wanted to make contact with her.'

'Well, she's with you a lot these days,' I said, and after a few more mumbled words I hurried away as fast as I could. I cried my eyes out all the way home.

What made it even more difficult was the fact that I had to go back. Jane was expecting a number of healing sessions and it would have been devastating for her to know there was no point. She so wanted to live. So I had to walk in with a smiling, carefree face and do whatever I could to ease her suffering.

The strain became so great that eventually I had to confide in Jane's sister, but I still returned regularly to the cheerful little house to go through the motions of healing. And I wasn't just pretending. I tried as hard as I possibly could to heal her. I prayed and prayed. But it was no use. The best I could hope for was to make Jane more comfortable, and give her peace of mind. I couldn't cure her.

A few months later she died, and it was as tragic as I knew it was going to be. The family were devastated, the poor children left motherless and I was bitter and angry with my guides.

'Why?' I kept asking them. 'Why did that have to happen? Why couldn't Jane stay?'

But there was no satisfactory answer.

Then some weeks later I was pottering about at home, my mind on other things, when I looked up and there was Jane standing in my living room, so beautiful it almost hurt to look at her. She'd always been pretty but now she was golden and shimmering with a pure light so dazzling it seared your eyes. She was an angel: 'an archangel in fact,' said Jane – which I believe is the highest kind.

'Stop these sad thoughts,' said Jane with a radiant smile. 'You must not give up healing. This is meant to be and I will help you.'

Since then, whenever I've started work on a difficult case I can sense Jane at my elbow and together we've achieved some wonderful successes.

The more different things I'm called upon to try, the

more amazed I am by this strange ability I seem to possess, and I'm increasingly curious about what it is and where it comes from. I suppose I've voiced these feelings rather too often at home because one day in 2005 Lisa looked into the kitchen, where I was stirring the family dinner on the stove, to say that she'd entered me for some kind of competition.

'It was advertised on the internet,' she said. 'They're looking for people to take part in a scientific challenge to test psychic powers. It's for a TV show. You're always saying you'd like to be tested scientifically so I applied for you.'

'You did WHAT?' I cried. 'What exactly do I have to do?'

'Dunno,' said Lisa. 'But it'll be cool. Anyway, must go. I'm off out tonight.' And she dashed out of the door before I could find out any more.

A little later I was invited to London for an interview and I began to learn more about the idea. Trisha Goddard was to be the presenter and the production company was whittling down 2,000 applicants to a final eight; these people would appear on screen over several weeks, taking part in a variety of tests. The lucky eight would not actually be paid, but they'd learn a great deal more about the nature of psychic phenomena. It sounded good to me.

At the studios the interviewees were given a number of tests similar to the exercises Jeff Marsh used to devise for the students he was nurturing. We had to guess what various envelopes contained and 'read' the faces in various photographs. At one point I recall holding a silver wedding ring and describing the owner and the house that went with it.

Afterwards, one of the production staff came up to me and said, 'I was a sceptic till I met you. But you've just described my house in great detail. That's remarkable.'

As I was leaving he called out to me, 'I hope to see you again.'

'It'll probably be in the car park,' I called back without thinking. But as I walked away I thought, whatever made you say that? What are you talking about – car park? He must think you're a bit stupid.

Despite this, I got through to the next round and was taken to a hotel where I was left alone in a room for about three hours. I didn't have anyone to talk to or anything to read, I didn't feel like watching TV and I was totally bored. Fortunately, there was a pad of paper on the table and I had a pen in my bag. I've never done much drawing before but I started to doodle. For some reason I drew lots of cars and a car park. The letters M.A.T wrote themselves in the corner and I sketched a car boot in more detail.

'Hmmm,' I thought when I'd finished. 'I'm not normally that interested in cars. This must be something to do with where we're going.'

Eventually, a taxi arrived to take me to our secret destination.

'Do you know where we're going?' asked the jovial Asian driver, ''cos I don't.'

'Well, they haven't told me,' I said, 'but I think we're going to a car park.'

'A car park? Why?'

'Search me,' I said.

Just then one of the TV crew jumped in.

'Hi,' he said, 'I'm Matt. I'm here to give directions to the driver. Okay, go to the end of the road and take a right, then straight on for about a hundred yards . . .' and on and on he went with some convoluted route.

Eventually we came to an open area with a building at the far end.

'Oh my God,' said the driver, 'this *is* a car park!'

I got out and looked across rows and rows of cars.

'Okay,' said Matt. 'Just walk about and see what you can find.'

The image of a very hot man squashed in a confined space flickered into my mind. Was I supposed to be looking for him? I walked up and down the lines of cars and suddenly Mark Green was beside me.

'What are you doing here, Mark?' I asked.

'Follow me,' he said, not answering my question. So I followed Mark, threading around the vehicles, and at one point I started to go into the undercover parking area by the building.

'You've just gone straight past,' said Mark. 'Come back and try this car here.'

And he stood by a vehicle with a pronounced boot.

I went back to it and put my hand on the lid.

'I think it's in here,' I said.

A crew member pressed the catch, the lid flew up and

inside was a man in a thick coat, sweating buckets. He uncoiled himself painfully and climbed out. 'Am I glad you found me,' he said, rubbing his cramped legs.

As I walked away the producer came over. It was the same man I'd predicted I'd meet in the car park. 'We meet again,' he said.

There were many more such tests spread over several weeks. It was a knockout contest and at the end of every programme the number of psychics was reduced. We were all used to working alone and being regarded as 'oddities' in our communities, so it was very good to meet other people like ourselves. We were on the same wavelength and I learned a tremendous amount from my fellow challengers. We were all sorry when yet another new friend had to leave just as we were getting to know each other.

One of the challenges I enjoyed most was finding a hidden child on a vast, windswept expanse of a Norfolk beach and sand dunes. The area extended for miles and the boy was actually hidden in a dip and covered over with sand and marram grass.

Before I arrived a sniffer dog had been assigned the task of finding him and so was the air–sea rescue team in the helicopter they use for real life emergencies similar to this. Apparently I located the boy faster than the dog, and the helicopter couldn't find him at all.

As I walked to the beach cousin Peter was saying in my ear: 'Left, left, left. Go left.'

So when I arrived I knew where I had to start and as I walked to the left, I saw an arrow on the horizon pointing downwards. I simply walked to the arrow and found the boy.

Everyone was amazed and I was very proud when the air–sea rescue team asked if they could call for my help in future, if ever they were having trouble finding someone who was lost.

'Of course,' I said.

A later test will, I hope, turn out to prove even more useful. I was taken to another rural lane, fringed by trees, and asked what I could pick up. Straight away I got an impression of a bubbly young girl who loved drama. I saw her walking along the lane and then there was a motorbike coming alongside her. I indicated the spot where it intercepted her. She was dead, that much was clear, but her body wasn't found in the lane, she told me.

She took me through the trees and out across a ploughed field. Trailing the camera crew behind me I plodded across the field until I came to a little spinney about half a mile away. But even that wasn't far enough. The girl was tugging me on, through the trees and down a slope to the edge of a pond concealed by the undergrowth.

'Here,' I said, standing by the water's edge, 'she was found here, half in and half out of the water and her nose and mouth were full of leaves.'

I went on to give them a description of the man the girl said was responsible, but this was not screened for legal reasons.

Afterwards they told me the details of the case.

Apparently a Norfolk teenager, pretty Johanna Young, had been murdered over ten years before. Her trainers and jeans had been found on the path where I'd stopped to mention the motorbike, but her body was recovered from the little wood across the ploughed field. She had a fractured skull, but her death was caused by drowning.

I'm told the police are examining the tapes of the programme to see if any new leads arise from the information.

The whole challenge was very hard work but immensely stimulating, and in February 2006 I was thrilled to hear that I'd won. I was presented with a mystical looking trophy of a face encased in glass and was awarded the title of Britain's Best Psychic – which made me very proud.

Peter, Lisa and Liam were delighted for me, and of course after that the phone didn't stop ringing. Newspapers, magazines, TV, radio: they all wanted to hear more and I was even asked to write a book.

For some reason it was the word 'book' that seemed to interest the Lined Man. Whenever I thought about it, I sensed him drawing close to me, and as I began work I realised how little I knew of my family background and African connections. So many of my father's relatives had now passed away. Only one, Uncle Leon's sister Girlie, still remained, and she was not in the best of health. She had once been the guardian of all the family documents and photographs, she told Mum. She couldn't remember much about it now, but she'd donated all the material, including a number of lions' heads, to the Oxford University Museum of Natural History.

That did it. As soon as Mum mentioned this to me I knew I had to go. The Lined Man was at my elbow, gently pushing me towards Oxford. I was busy: Liam was starting a new school, there was so much to do, but the Lined Man would give me no peace until I made an appointment with the curator of the museum to go and look at the Preston file.

Mum and I drove up there one drizzly day in October. I'd never been to Oxford before and it was thrilling to arrive in that beautiful city amongst all those ancient stone buildings. The museum appeared just as venerable and lovely as the others and the curator, a surprisingly young woman in tweedy academic clothes, led us through a maze of winding corridors far from the public quarters to what looked like a laboratory at the back. There were dozens and dozens of tortoise shells in the process of being labelled and a number of fossils lying about.

'Here you are,' said the curator with a smile, handing us a bulging file. 'It's all in here.'

The Lined Man was so close I could almost feel him breathing down my neck.

There were letters, the manuscript of a book written by my great, great-grandfather about the building of the railway through Kenya and a pile of old, faded photographs.

I picked up the photographs. There was dear old

Uncle Leon, a handsome young man in army uniform, slim and dark with a dashing pencil moustache and big brown eyes. There was great-aunt Girlie, an attractive young woman with clouds of soft hair and a gentle smile. There were lions and elephants striding the plains, a poster advertising the new-fangled Ford cars recently launched in Kenya and there was an indistinct little group on the banks of a lake with a pretty woman in the foreground wearing big leg-of-mutton sleeves and holding a hammer aloft. It was Florence, just about to knock the last rail into place at the spot which became Port Florence.

And finally there was a distinguished white-haired man sitting on the wooden steps of a tropical verandah. He had a strong, angular face, haunting eyes and a complexion deeply scored from the harsh African sun.

I recognised him immediately. It was the Lined Man. My great, great-grandfather, Ronald Owen Preston.

'Look at this, Mum!' I said, handing her the picture.

'Oh my God,' said Mum. 'That's the man you were always talking about isn't it? With the lined face? Ever since you were a little girl. And I thought you were making up stories. Well I'm blowed.'

She'd never seen him before, no-one remaining in the family had ever seen him, but she recognised him immediately from my past descriptions.

I stared deep into those dark, familiar eyes for a long, long time. Then with shaking hands I picked up the next item. It was a letter from my great, great grandfather to his son. 'Son, dear,' it began. 'This is true history which will interest you. It was just five years after the great Indian Mutiny that a party left England taking the Overland Route, which meant paddle boat from Dover to Calais, train from Calais to Brindisi . . .'

And he went on to recount how his father, David Preston, came to meet his mother Emma en route for India and how he himself was born and grew up to work as an engineer on the railways there, before moving on and taking his expertise to Africa and the country that was one day to become Kenya. The letter was signed R.O. Preston and dated February 7 1946.

As I read the trials and tribulations of Ronald's childhood – he was orphaned and then abandoned at one point – I felt moved to tears. I could picture him as a little boy in shorts in that distant land and my heart went out to him. The Lined Man's presence seemed to fill the whole room as the closely-typed words blurred before my eyes and I sensed a great contentment washing over me. He was happy that I'd found him at last and had learned a little about the lost story of our family.

Now I understood why he'd kept the secret of his identity from me for all these years. No family history whispered in my ear would have had the same impact as holding the letter written by his own hand, or seeing his face captured as it used to be in that old photograph. Had I known from the beginning who he was, I would also have known something of our family, or thought I did, and curiosity might never have driven me to Oxford to seek out more. Those old pictures, the letters and the knowledge that they even existed, might have been lost to us forever. And I would never truly have known the Lined Man. What's more, my mother would never have had the proof she needed that he existed outside my head.

The Lined Man interrupted my thoughts. 'Your generation can ease a lot of pain,' I heard him say. 'The veil is lifting and I bring you evidence of life. This is only the beginning . . .'